CONTROLLING LIQUOR, WINE, & BEVERAGE COSTS

By Elizabeth Godsmark

The Food Service Professionals Guide To:
Controlling Liquor, Wine & Beverage Costs: 365
Secrets Revealed

Atlantic Publishing Group, Inc. Copy right © 2003
1210 SW 23rd. Place
Ocala, Florida 34474
800.541.1336
352-622-5836 - Fax

www.atlantic-pub.com - Web Site
sales@atlantic-pub.com E-mail

SAN Number :268-1250

International Standard Book Number: 0-910627-18-5

Library of Congress Cataloging-in-Publication Data

Brown, Douglas Robert, 1960-
Reducing liquor, wine & beverage costs : 365 secrets revealed
by Douglas Robert Brown.
p. cm. -- (The food service professionals guide to ; 8)
Includes bibliographical references and index.
ISBN 0-910627-18-5 (pbk. : alk. paper)
1. Bartending. 2. Food service management.   I. Title. II.
Title:Reducing liquor, wine, and beverage costs. III. Series.
TX950.7.B76 2003
641.8'74--dc21

2002011169

Printed in Canada

Book layout and design by Meg Buchner of Megadesign
www.mega-designs.com • e-mail: megadesn@mhtc.net

CONTENTS

7. DRINK SELECTION

8. STAFF RECRUITMENT, MANAGEMENT & TRAINING

9. OTHER OPPORTUNITIES TO CONTROL COSTS IN THE BEVERAGE INDUSTRY

INTRODUCTION

You're busy. You just don't have the time to wade through a pile of "heavy" manuals on how to reduce liquor, wine and beverage costs. But you do need answers and you need them FAST! You want instant solutions; practical ideas, tips and suggestions that you can implement NOW.

Look no further. *Controlling Liquor, Wine & Beverage Costs: 365 Secrets Revealed* has done the job for you. It contains a wealth of inspiration and practical advice that can help reduce costs and boost profits in any beverage operation. Implement just a handful of these suggestions and transform your establishment into a thriving and successful enterprise. All it takes is a few simple and quick actions to turn things round!

Worried about cash flow, staff problems, inventory control, theft or any of the myriad of problems that plague the beverage industry? The pitfalls are many. But so, too, are the opportunities. Accept the challenge and take a few shortcuts to success.

Cheers!

Every business needs to budget— including bars.

CHAPTER ONE

BUDGETING & FORECASTING

Grasp the Basics about Budgeting

Don't be put off by all the jargon and terminology associated with budgeting. Oftentimes, a simple overview is all you need to make a big difference in the profitability of your establishment. Consider the following:

- **Budgeting in a nutshell.** All it involves is planning for income, expense and profit. Simply bear in mind all three aspects of budgeting when making important business decisions.

- **Establish an operating budget.** This is a basic plan that estimates what sales income will be generated and what expenses can be incurred in order to meet profit targets. Choose from a variety of different types of budgets, such as long- and short-term, cash and capital. The short, one-year operational budget is probably best suited to a beverage operation.

- **Use your budget plan to reduce costs.** For example, when sales fall below forecast levels, or when expenses exceed budget estimates, do something about it, immediately! Review recent expenditures or consider a sales promotion.

- **Use your budget plan to establish standards.**
  Consistent quality is one of the surest ways to
  boost profits. Don't compromise on quality in an
  attempt to achieve sales goals.

- **Use your budget plan to establish benchmarks
  for expenditure.** Your budget plan is a useful tool
  for reviewing general expenditure. Use it. Take a
  fresh look at other aspects of expenditure, such as
  labor and energy costs.

Choose the Right Budget Plan for Your Business

No beverage operation can survive without an effective
budget plan. It provides more than a useful
evaluative tool for management. It is essential for
keeping operation costs within budget limits and is a
good indicator of which areas of the operation require
immediate corrective action. There are three main types
of budget: fixed, flexible and zero-based. Each, however,
follows the same broad, two-stage procedure.

- **The two stages.** It is well worth following this broad
  two-stage outline. It gives structure to your budget.
  The first stage is known as "descriptive." It deals with
  assumptions only. These assumptions are then used
  to develop the second stage of the plan, the financial
  aspect, which goes into much greater depth.

- **Fixed budget.** Fixed budgets assume that expenses
  and sales volume will remain stable during the twelve-
  month period. Fixed budgets are useful for evaluating
  past costs and performance.

- **Flexible budget.** Sales in the beverage industry tend
  to fluctuate considerably. A flexible budget is useful in

this type of situation where, in order for profitability to be maintained, costs need to be re-assessed at frequent intervals.

- **Zero-based budget.** The zero-based budget is a variation on the flexible budget. Although costs are estimated within a range of activities, the starting point for developing costs for the new budget is always zero. This is useful in operations, such as liquor outlets, where accountability is essential.

- **Finally, whatever your choice of plan, don't complicate matters!** Only include information in your budget plan that is useful and relevant to your particular establishment.

Adapt Your Chosen Budget Plan to Suit Your Establishment

Having established the need for a budget (there's no getting away from it!) and decided upon which method best suits your establishment, you now need to put some thought into personalizing and adapting your chosen budget plan. Think flexibility, and make your budget work for you.

- **Keep it simple.** For example, if you manage a single-unit operation, concentrate on recording only basic budgetary information. Even if you are responsible for running a multiunit operation that involves budgeting for several operations, the plan need not be complex. Review current procedures and eliminate any details that are not essential to the smooth running of your operation.

- **Delegate.** In small operations, the owner has little choice but to develop and operate the budget single-handedly. However, if you run a larger establishment, delegate! Assign budget management to specific members of personnel.

- **Consult.** Use budget analysis as an opportunity to consult with other members of staff. Have a brain-storming session. Each employee can offer a different perspective about where and how to trim costs.

- **Introduce "bottom-up" budgeting.** Most employees, from the most junior upwards, prefer to be involved in the company's budgeting strategy, rather than be subject to "top-down" budgeting, where all decisions are made at the corporate level.

Budget Control - Introduce Cost-Effective Initiatives

The budget manager is responsible for developing cost-controlling policies throughout the operation. An effective budget should enable you to control costs and improve overall efficiency. Budgeting solutions need to be easy to apply, suitable and ethical. For optimum results, focus on the following areas:

- **Financial reports.** These are the building blocks of successful budgeting. Consolidate daily, weekly and monthly figures. Ask questions. Investigate, for example, whether certain products are more profitable than others and whether wastage is too high in certain areas.

- **Labor productivity controls.** Within budget resources, now may be the time to introduce pro-ductivity improvements. Could you automate inventory, purchasing, requisitioning and issuing procedures? Maybe review employee insurance policies - are you getting the best value for your money?

- **Maintain company assets.** Get the most out of your computer systems, particularly those designed for purchasing, inventory and bar support. Are these systems being used to their full capacities? Seek advice about upgrading.

- **Protect your establishment from unnecessary exposure.** Of course budgetary controls must be cost-effective, but beware of overstepping the mark. Any cost-cutting initiatives must comply with Internal Revenue Service (IRS) legislation, safety laws and any other labor regulations that may apply to your business.

Develop a Forecasting Strategy That Is Relevant and Realistic

Company forecasts are often unusable for the simple reason that they contain too much irrelevant information. "Blanket" forecasting that is relevant only in parts to your operation often renders the whole report redundant. Devise a forecasting plan that is 100-percent useful to your establishment.

- **Basic requirements.** Forecasts should focus on two main areas only:
    1. Operational issues - e.g., purchasing and staffing.
    2. Financial results - e.g., estimated costs and revenue percentages.

  Any other figures are of limited value.

- **Minimum information requirements.** All you need to establish any type of budget is the following information:
    1. Previous period operating figures.
    2. Assumptions of next period operations.
    3. Targets.
    4. Simple monitoring procedures.

- **Forecasting methods.** There are several methods of forecasting available, many of them time-consuming and unproductive. Pause first and ask yourself three simple questions:
    1. Is the method practical?
    2. Will the end results be reliable?
    3. Is this method cost-effective?

    Choose your method according to your answers.

- **Analysis.** Stick to basics. Successful forecasting is simply a matter of predicting the consequences of certain business decisions over a specific period of time.

- **Time.** In most operations, time is a prime consideration. Make sure that any time spent on forecasting is used constructively. Focus on achieving tangible results, like trimming costs in areas such as inventory, labor and/or operations.

- **Resources.** Does your establishment have the resources to implement your chosen forecasting method: are data readily available?

Make Forecasting Work for Your Establishment

Forecasting is traditionally associated with the obligatory exercise of producing figures for bank managers or accountants. It need not, however, be unproductive. Turn forecasting into a useful predictor of your operation's future performance. Use it as a tool in the planning process. Make it an integral part of budget strategy. Consider the following possibilities:

- **Sales team approach.** Get sales personnel involved with producing forecasts for their own sections of the operation. Responsibility promotes accuracy and increased employee commitment.

- **Identify problems sooner rather than later.** Use forecasts to alert management to weaknesses in specific areas of the operation. Take action immediately to remedy, for instance, inventory discrepancies behind the bar.

- **Clientele expectations.** An underused yet highly effective approach to forecasting. Devise customer surveys. Value the opinions of all those who patronize your establishment.

- **Executive opinion.** In large enterprises, forecasting often centers on the collective opinion of top executives from the various divisions including sales, purchasing and accounting. Adopt this approach to forecasting if you want representative, accurate and rapid feedback, as well as workable solutions.

- **Labor forecasting.** Use sales forecasts to establish required labor. Overstaffing, for even a single shift, can considerably reduce profits.

Budgeting and Beyond - Look to the Future

There are those who argue that a budget isn't necessary; that it's too time-consuming, too revealing, that it causes conflict. Many established enterprises, however, are convinced that they would not be in business today if it were not for sound budgeting and, more specifically, long-range budgeting. Adopt a long-term approach.

- **Achievement budget.** This short-term budget covers a brief period, say a week or a month. It includes information such as weekly bar requisition totals and the number of staff required for the seven-day period. But, as the achievement budget is the foundation for long-range budgeting, it is vital to get it right from the start.

- **Annual budget.** Most enterprises that operate a budget do so on a yearly basis. Project ahead, beyond this period's end. Identify long-term trends and make them work for you.

- **Long-range budget.** Devise a three- to-five-year budget (sometimes referred to as a strategic plan). All you need to produce is a brief outline about where the operation should be heading. For example, you may want to add extra operational units to increase sales, or maybe you're planning a construction project that could temporarily restrict sales volume.

Computerized Budgeting and Forecasting

There's no getting away from it, when it comes to budgeting and forecasting, a computer is the backbone of most beverage operations. All you need is an electronic spreadsheet, such as Microsoft Excel. Most small establishments need look no further. However, packages, tailormade to the industry's requirements, have become increasingly popular over the years for both routine and advanced applications. Here are a few pointers to help you choose the system that is right for your establishment:

- **Basic electronic spreadsheet software.** These programs are specifically designed to cope with all types of budgeting and forecasting. They are low-cost and simple in concept. The electronic spreadsheet looks like a traditional worksheet; arranged in rows and columns and is straightforward to use. And, it has powerful computation capabilities that do all the time-consuming, routine calculations for you!

- **Customize your spreadsheet.** Use your spreadsheet to set up a simple budgetary model that exactly reflects your establishment's budget plan. Once it's set up, all you have to do is change a few numbers each time you update the spreadsheet. Stick to the relevant. On other hand, you may get carried away by the range of opportunity offered for refining your budget - in which case, explore the possibilities! The scope for cost trimming can be quite a revelation!

- **Graphs and charts at the click of a button.**
  When presenting budgets and forecasts to other
  people, using a visual approach is often more
  effective. Use your spreadsheet to display your
  information graphically.

- **Multiunit operations.** Larger enterprises may be
  better off with software aimed specifically at the
  beverage industry. Investigate the following
  suppliers:

  QuickPlan
  www.atlantic-pub.com 800-541-1336

  Synergy International
  www.synergy-intl.com..................800-522-6210

  Caterware
  www.caterware.com 800-853-1017

Cost-Volume-Profit (CVP) Analysis - The Key to Budgetary Success

One of the simplest ways of performing budget
analysis is the cost-volume-profit method.
Sometimes referred to as "breakeven," this is
fundamental budgetary analysis. Budget analysts need
to do more than just review the links between costs,
sales, volumes and profits; they should constantly be on
the lookout for alternative ways of reducing costs and
boosting profits. Ask yourself the following questions,
and use simple graphs to illustrate your points:

- **Profit goals.** How many drinks does this establishment need to serve in order meet budgeted profit
  targets?

- **Cost increases.** When variable and fixed costs increase, how many extra drinks will we have to serve in order to maintain budgeted profit targets?

- **Opening hours/quiet periods.** Is it worth considering expanding opening hours? Would it be profitable? Or should the outlet remain open during predictably quiet "drinking" times?

- **Balance and perspective.** Get it right. Too rigid an application of CVP findings can be counterproductive. You can't risk losing guest goodwill and employee support. Too heavy-handed an approach can cause your profits to plummet!

- **CVP software.** Check out this low-cost software tool for CVP analysis:

  - **CVP Optimizer** - available from several online software retailers, including ZD Net (www.zdnet.com), 32 Bit (www.32bit.com) and Virtual Software (www.virtualsoftware.com).

Monitoring Your Budget Plan

An operational budget plan is no good if you don't use it. Sound complicated? It doesn't have to be. Simply focus on three main areas for maximum benefit: income, expense and profit:

- **Income.** Income falling below projected levels? Do you feel that you're busier than ever but sales volumes aren't increasing? Select from a handful of alternative strategies without delay. For example, are you overstaffed, overstocked, selling the right drinks, pitching markup too low? The bottom line is: if sales volumes are lower than originally projected, management must immediately take measures to increase income.

- **Expense.** Just as it isn't always easy to predict future sales volumes accurately, it isn't easy to estimate future expenses either. Income varies, and so does expense. One way to avoid too many nasty shocks is to use a "yardstick" method to determine expense "standards." Simply compare budgeted expense performance with actual performance, over several volume levels. Apply this yardstick method to stock, labor and general expenditure.

- **Profit: Income - Expense = Profit.**
  Or, more specifically, Budgeted income - budgeted expense = budgeted profit. Budgeted profit must be realized if your operation is going to survive. The solution is to protect (at all costs) your operational income by constantly investigating alternatives in all areas of the operation.

CHAPTER TWO

COSTING, MARGINS & CASH CONTROL

The Basic Mathematics of Profitability

A typical beverage operation generates a constant stream of data and information, endless columns of figures and daily records. But you'd be surprised how few managers actually do anything with these figures, let alone fully grasp their implications. So how can you tell if you're operating profitably? The answer is you can't, unless, of course, you get to grips with some basic mathematics. For a start, you'll need to know how to perform a few simple calculations, such as working out an item's cost percentage. You don't need to be a mathematician to figure the following straightforward formulas:

- **Cost per ounce.** This is the basic unit cost of a drink. For example, to calculate the cost per ounce of a liter bottle, divide the wholesale cost of the bottle by 33.8 ounces, or in the case of a 750ml bottle, by 25.4 ounces. The figure you arrive at is the cost per ounce.

- **Cost per portion.** To be able to price a certain drink, you must first calculate the base cost of the serving. Use the cost per ounce to work out the cost per portion. For example, if the cost per ounce is $0.60 and the recipe requires 1.5 ounces, then the portion cost is $0.90.

- **Cost percentage.** Master this formula. You cannot function without it! To calculate the cost percentage of an item, divide the product's cost (or portion's cost) by its sale price and then multiply by 100. This simple calculation gives you the cost percentage. Profitability hangs on this key calculation. This calculation is the most frequently used formula in the beverage industry. It indicates the profit margin of any drink and represents the difference between the cost of the item and the price for which it is sold. If cost percentage increases, profit margins decrease.

Measuring Bottle Yield

You know the theory: to obtain the cost per ounce, you must divide the cost of the bottle by the number of ounces in the bottle. Fine, so far. But sometimes, in practice, the final sales volumes and profits can seem disappointing. You're confused because you have done everything by the book, and now, somehow, the figures don't quite add up. Get wise.

- **Consider evaporation and spillage.** When calculating a bottle's cost per ounce, the secret is to deduct an ounce or two up front, before dividing, to allow for evaporation or spillage. Although this will slightly increase the cost per ounce, it will also give you a more realistic starting point.

- **Calculation errors.** Slight variations can easily creep into a calculation involving both liters and ounces. For example, assume a highball contains 1-1/2 ounces of spirit (or 45ml): using ounces, a liter bottle yields 22.54 measures, whereas, using milliliters, the bottle gives 22.22 measures. Tip:

"round down" in the interests of reality.

- **Maximize potential yield**. You know that a bottle of liquor yields so many measures at a certain cost. However, you also know that sloppy pouring methods can wipe out potential profits. The best way to overcome this problem is to automate portion serving as much as possible. You've paid for the liquor and want maximum returns.

- **Buy big.** High-turnover liquor, wines and spirits should always be purchased in larger bottles for better yield per measure.

Drink Pricing for Optimum Profits

Sensitive pricing can make or break your operation. Pricing decisions should never, ever, be made arbitrarily. It is crucial to achieve that fine balance between pricing for optimum profits and making customers feel that they're getting value for money. Of course, you want to sell the drinks at their optimum sales volume, but if you tip the balance by raising the sales price too high, the sales volume will actually drop. So will the profits.

- **Research target audience.** Investigate your potential market. Check out the opposition, even if this means visiting every liquor outlet in your locality. Get a feel for how much guests are prepared to pay for certain types of drinks.

- **Compete.** A realistic view of market positioning is essential. Aim to match, beat or pitch for exclusivity (known as a "highball decision", in the beverage industry). All three methods can work.

What won't work is a "muddling along" approach. Make a decision, set your goals and price accordingly.

- **Type of operation.** Customers' image and perception of your establishment play a major role in establishing a pricing structure. Guests have fixed expectations about costs. For example, they expect to pay above-average price at a smart nightclub or "adult" establishment. They expect neighborhood bars, on the other hand, to be cheaper. Devise a pricing strategy that meets customer expectations.

- **Portion costs.** You may have done your research and drawn up the perfect plan to wipe out the opposition, but, if you haven't "bought in" at competitive prices, you're not going to win. Keep portion costs to a minimum by buying low.

Take a Fresh Look at How You Apply Your Pricing Strategy

Having carefully considered all aspects of your pricing strategy, including cost, availability, competition and target audience, it is essential to make your pricing plan as user-friendly and easy to operate as possible. Simplify.

- **Price lists.** A complicated price list with too many options and variables leads to employee confusion and incorrect charging. Even if those errors result in higher gross sales, customers will soon complain and you will lose business.

- **Devise main price categories.** Group products according to their wholesale costs. Use standard increments, like 50 cents, to separate price categories.

- **Keep drink prices based on quarters.** Prices ending in quarters - $0.25, $0.50 and $0.75 - are easier for bartenders to add up mentally.

- **List product prices with their corresponding specific portion size**. For example, alongside each item in the liquor inventory, list the appropriate portion size for that drink.

- **Point-of-sale system.** Make bartenders' lives a whole lot easier! Invest in an automated system, where a few keystrokes are all that's required to find any drink or item on the price list. For more information about POS systems, contact:

   Action Systems
   www.actionsystems.com 800-356-6037

   Vital Link
   www.vitallink.com 877-770-7795

   Canfield POS
   www.possales.com..........................502-456-2299

Markups - Where to Pitch It

There are no standard markup guidelines in the beverage industry. Unfortunately, getting it right is very important. Profitability, cost control and so much more hang upon those difficult markup decisions. Here are a few guidelines to point you in the right direction:

- **Broad guidelines.** You need to start somewhere. The following markup suggestions may help:

  Cocktails ....3 $1/2$- 4 times cost
  Other liquor ....4 - 5 times cost
  Beer ....2 $1/2$- 3 times cost
  Wine by the glass ....3 - 4 times cost
  Carafe wine ....2 $1/2$- 3 times cost
  Dessert wines ....2 - 2$1/2$ times cost

  Based on the above markup guidelines, the total beverage cost is approximately 28 percent.

- **Three main pricing methods.** There are, however, three general approaches to markups in the beverage industry. A basic understanding of these options will guide you in the right direction:

  1. Traditional markup - a combination of intuition and local competition. Don't rely on intuition alone - you'd be on to a loser.

  2. Cost plus markup - here, price is determined by adding a markup to the cost of the item. Easy to apply, this method is popular in the beverage industry.

  3. Item cost percentage markup - similar to cost plus pricing, but linked to profit targets.

- **Type of establishment.** Markup is often driven by the type of establishment. For example, luxury hotels, restaurants and nightclubs can command heftier markups. Bars and taverns, on the other hand, have to compete more fiercely with similar outlets in the locality.

Bar Cash-Control Procedures

Cash flow, in the bar trade, means just that: cash. It is a cash-dominated environment, and that cash needs to carefully controlled. It is the beverage manager's responsibility to make sure that all cash receipts end up where they should be - in the cash register. Establish strict cash-handling procedures. It's the only way to survive in the industry, make a profit and keep costs under control.

- **On-hand cash.** Record the "house bank" total at the beginning and end of every shift. Make the opening bartender responsible for counting it. Keep the on-hand cash in a separate, secure drawer behind the bar. Never let the closing bartender total his or her own end-of-shift bank.

- **Random spot-checks.** Introduce impromptu cash counts - by the manager. Keep bar staff on their toes!

- **Count cash when you are least likely to be disturbed.** Be aware of the possibility of distractions and NEVER leave cash unattended, even for just a few seconds.

- **Opening bank** - the amount of cash in the register at the beginning of a shift. Make sure staff have enough cash in each denomination, thus removing the need to leave the register unattended during business hours.

- **Security.** Keep opening banks in bags in the office safe until required by the bartender. Staff must always verify and sign for the amount. Closing banks should follow the same strict procedures.

Tighten Up Daily Cash Procedures

Fact: improved daily control of cash leads to lower costs and increased profits. Monitor cash at every stage throughout the operation - daily. One weak link is enough to wipe out the entire business. The sequence of activities will vary according to the size and type of beverage outlet. Certain procedures, however, are common to all establishments:

- **Routine.** It may sound dull, but sticking to repetitive procedures is the best way of making sure that no link in the daily cash cycle is overlooked.

- **Complete count of reserve cash.** Do this daily. Include cash from the opening bank, plus on-hand cash. It's a good idea to count on-hand cash after the bank deposit has been completed. This gives you tighter control because the sales cash already will have been counted.

- **Assign register drawers to specific shifts.** Separate drawers protect the honest employee and disclose the dishonest. Include the adding machine printout with the opening bank.

- **Remove all large bills at intervals during each shift.** Place them in the safe.

- **Take a "Z" reading of the cash register at the end of each shift.** Remove both the drawer and the "Z" reading from the bar. Take them to the office.

- **Reconcile all cash in a secure environment.** This is essential.

- **Bevinco Auditing Services.** Investigate this powerful cash control tool. A software package aimed at the beverage industry, it offers independent, precise monitoring of bar inventory. Contact Bevinco, 250 Consumers Road, Suite 1103, Toronto, Ontario, Canada, M2J 4V6, www.bevinco.com.

- **Audit Net.** Free beverage audit resources are available on the Audit Net website at www.audit.net.

Take the Hassle out of Cash Reconciliation

Save time and money by introducing simple step-by-step cash reconciliation procedures. The process should be the same whether you're handling cash from a point-of-sale system or a cash register. The following ten-point guideline will help. It summarizes the information (no more, no less) that you need to record for the purposes of cash reconciliation:

1. Count and record all the cash in the cash drawer. Enter each denomination in a separate column of the cash drawer reconciliation form. Also, enter a grand total for all coins.

2. Enter the total amount of credit card sales.

3. Enter the total amount of check sales.

4. Record non-beverage merchandise sales in a separate column.

5. Enter all cash paid out for miscellaneous purchases in another column.

6.   Next, enter the subtotals for cash, credit cards, checks, other sales and "paid outs."

7.   Create the "opening bank" for the next shift. Record the total, and place the opening bank in the safe.

8.   Subtract the amount of the opening bank from the subtotal to arrive at the total "accountable funds" for the shift.

9.   Enter this figure in the final column of the cash drawer reconciliation form.

10.   Last, record the gross sales figure for the register's "Z" report. Positive figures mean that the total is "over"; negative, that it is "under" or short. This figure is the final figure that you need to enter on the reconciliation form.

Gross Profits - The Lowdown

There is no better indicator of a business's success than its gross profit figure. By definition, gross profit is the cash difference between an item or portion cost and its sales price. All attempts to reduce costs should focus on this gross profit figure. Get to grips with how to figure out some important calculations related to gross profits.

- **Gross profit.** To calculate a drink's gross profit, simply subtract its portion cost from its sale price.

- **Gross profit margin.** This figure represents the percentage amount of profit made by the sale. Divide the amount of profit by the sales price and then multiply by 100. The result is the gross profit margin.

- **Sales percentage profits.** To calculate the selling price (based on the required gross profit margin), divide the portion cost by the gross profit margin percentage "reciprocal," i.e., the figure you get from subtracting the target gross margin from 100.

- **Cost multiplier.** This calculation is often used in the beverage industry to figure out the target selling price for a drink based on its portion cost. Divide the cost percentage you require by 100 and then multiply the result by the portion cost of the product.

- **Mixed-drink prime ingredient costing.** A calculation used to determine the target sales price for a mixed drink that has only one main ingredient, such as gin and tonic or scotch on the rocks. All you have to do is divide the drink's portion cost by the target cost percentage.

Common Cash Control Problems - Troubleshooting

You notice that the pouring costs (PC) are escalating, but you can't figure out why. Check out the following possibilities and take measures to recover the situation:

- **Have liquor costs risen, but your prices remained the same?** Cover costs immediately. You need to up the drink prices to match. But don't price yourself out of the market.

- **Not sure whether to include tax in your pricing?** Confused over how to handle the small cash denominations generated by tax charges? Having to hand over small change on each purchase can really annoy customers and bartenders alike. Set your prices at a round level and include the tax in the price.

- **Sales volume decreasing?** First take a look at the competition. You may not have been keeping tabs on competitors' prices or promotions. Remember, their liquor costs are pretty similar to yours.

- **Does the slump in business coincide with taking on new bar staff?** Check whether they are pouring drinks correctly and following drink recipe guides. Review daily figures to see if the PC is higher on shifts when a particular staff member is on duty.

- **Are sales down despite an increase in the number of bottles requisitioned from stock?** Be wary. Perhaps members of staff are taking advantage: either drinking on the job or thieving.

- **Problems outside of business hours?** Inventory discrepancies? First suspect dishonest activities. Narrow down which personnel might have been on the premises while the establishment was closed. Investigate further.

- **It still doesn't add up?** Check out the following: Are employees giving away drinks to friends? Are bartenders overpouring? (In which case, change from free-pouring to more controlled pouring methods.) Go back to basics and double-check shipment totals against invoices.

CHAPTER THREE

PURCHASING

Customize a Buying Strategy That Reduces Costs

Do you have a purchasing strategy? If not, you need one - NOW! It's never too late. A good buying plan is one of the quickest (and easiest) ways to reduce costs and make sure that your establishment gets the most for its money. Remember, the best place to control costs is in the purchasing department. The plan doesn't have to be complicated - just well thought out and straightforward to implement. A few bulleted points will do. Keep your plan simple and stick to it.

- **Use a simple five-prong purchasing strategy.** You want to buy:
  - The right product
  - Of the right quality
  - At the right price
  - At the right time
  - From the right source

- **Think of purchasing as a cycle, not a one-off activity.** Purchasing is not just a matter of phoning or e-mailing through another order. You don't want to run out, nor do you want to overstock.

- **Purchasing is not a separate activity.** What, how and when you buy must always (yes, always!)

reflect the overall goals of your establishment. Trends change - so must you, the purchaser.

- **Commit your purchasing strategy in writing.** Write your plan down on paper; save it on your computer, or any place where it is easily accessible. You never know when other members of staff will need to deputize.

- **Step back.** Get an overview. Ask yourself whether you're buying on the basis of long-term fixed prices or current market prices. You should be doing both.

Tighten Up Your Purchasing Procedures

Although it's not always the easiest thing to do when you're busy, the introduction of even a few basic "tightening up" procedures can make the purchasing manager's life a whole lot easier - and reduce costs!

- **Use your written purchasing strategy as a step-by-step guide.** It saves time and money in the long run. Even if you are 100 percent familiar with your establishment's current purchasing procedures, it's all too easy to overlook a crucial link in the procedure and end up wasting time backtracking or duplicating effort.

- **Reassess your timing techniques.** Timing is crucial. Tune in to the drinks' market price fluctuations. The wine industry in particular is prone to seasonal fluctuations. Also consider the bulk buying of soft drinks in anticipation of the summer season.

- **Review your purchasing schedule regularly.**
  Consumption of liquor, wines and beverages
  fluctuates, from month to month and year to year.
  A buying pattern that worked well last year may be
  be way off the mark today. Consider whether it is
  better to buy daily, weekly, or in the case of
  certain drinks, monthly.

- **Take a fresh look at the layout of your
  purchase order.** Is it accurately laid out, and are
  your instructions easy to follow? Remove any
  ambiguity - and remove the unnecessary hassle of
  processing "returns."

- **Check out your vendors.** Do they have a good
  track record for quality and reliability? Are they
  easy to deal with when things go wrong? Update
  your vendor contact list regularly, and always
  remain alert to possible new suppliers. Keep
  existing vendors on their toes!

Buy Quality

The quality of the merchandise purchased sets the
tone and standards for the whole establishment.
Don't leave quality to chance. Mistakes can be
expensive. Word spreads fast and you want a good
reputation!

- **Be up-front about quality.** Make a conscious
  decision to purchase "quality" merchandise at the
  stage when the goals of the business are being
  established.

- **The products you are buying must be suitable
  for their intended use.** Studies have proven that
  the more suitable a product, the higher its quality.

Make sure that the quality of any product measures up to the needs of your establishment.

- **Quality must apply throughout the establishment.** When it comes to quality, don't concentrate on alcohol beverages alone. Of course the types of wines, spirits, beers and liqueurs you sell are all crucially important; but don't forget the non-alcoholic beverages, such as quality coffee and soft drinks. Consumers in this sector of the market are a discerning and vociferous bunch! Something as simple as a poor cup of coffee can drive a customer away, never to return.

- **Don't compromise on quality.** Don't be distracted by poor-quality "offers" or bulk buys that you think, on the spur of the moment, might just "do." They won't. You'll end up regretting the purchase.

- **Evaluate each product's quality in relation to cost.** The most expensive product is not necessarily the best product for your enterprise. When making purchasing decisions, there is no need to sacrifice quality.

- **Look at quality from a clientele perspective.** What level of quality do your guests expect? Meet their requirements.

- **Review your vendors for quality.** Do you suffer from wastage due to poor quality products? Assess the quality level of potential vendors by first asking for samples. Document quality specifications to vendors. It is important to avoid misunderstandings.

A Good Purchasing Security System Can Save You Big Bucks

Build security into your purchasing procedures. The choice of security system, however, depends a lot upon the size of your operation. If you are the "head cook and bottle washer" of a small establishment, security is a much simpler issue. If, however, you are part of a larger enterprise where a number of personnel are involved in purchasing, then security becomes a major concern. If this is your lot, give the following issues serious consideration:

- **Set up a reliable purchasing control system.** Whether your chosen system is manually operated or computerized, it must be free from loopholes. There are several good-value computerized packages available on the market today that are specifically designed for the liquor and beverage industry. Most of these packages offer a range of built-in security features. Get more information at:

  Atlantic Publishing
  www.atlantic-pub.com....................800-541-1366

  Cash Trrap
  www.trrap.com 515-957-8478

  Food-Trak
  www.foodtrak.com..........................800-553-2438

- **Beware of bogus documentation.** Make sure that routine purchasing procedures are accurately documented from start to finish. Attention to detail in this area will help alert you to breaches of security. Be constantly on the lookout for calculation "errors," deliberate duplication, "incorrect" invoices and bogus credit requests. These are all common ploys used by unscrupulous purchasers and vendors.

- **Beware of the possibility of kickbacks.** Some
buyers have been known to "work" with suppliers
in return for benefits such as money or gifts.
Unfortunately, it happens all too often. Such
"practiced" buyers and sellers are often masters of
disguise, so don't be green, be keen!

- **Beware of purchaser theft.** This can take several
forms. Purchasers may order merchandise for their
own personal use or they may buy wholesale with
the intent to "selling on." A carefully designed
purchasing system will take care of most of these
problems.

Keep Purchasing Procedures Simple

Whatever the size of your operation, certain repetitive
purchasing procedures are unavoidable. At the
very minimum, a buyer has to complete a purchasing
requisition, a purchase order, a shipping instruction, a
receiving report and carry out some form of quality
control. Purchasing procedures, however, exist for a
good reason. Save time, effort and money by simplifying
them.

- **Change your attitude.** Instead of viewing
purchasing procedures as an irritation, think of
them as a support system. Accurate documentation in this area has rescued many a business
from the jaws of liquidation.

- **Concentrate on basics.** Buyers should always
have adequate purchasing procedures in place.
The key, however, is to avoid overkill. If a certain

procedure in the buying cycle is irrelevant to your establishment, get rid of it. A written requisition, for example, may not be necessary if you regularly "call off" stock ordered on a contract basis. Adapt and be flexible.

- **The purchasing requisition.** Save time. Establish a pared-down requisition procedure that identifies ongoing requirements and automatically triggers the purchasing cycle.

- **The purchase order.** No skimping here! The purchase order is a legal contract between purchaser and vendor. Even in small organizations, the purchase order needs to be put in writing. Get it right. It can save time, hassle and money in the long run. A computer-generated purchase order considerably reduces human error.

- **The shipping instruction.** Keep it simple. This piece of documentation is merely a confirmation of instructions from the buyer to the seller. Whether handwritten or computerized, the shipping instruction needs only to contain simple information. It should include the purchase order number for the shipment, and it, too, should be numbered for record-keeping purposes.

- **The receiving report.** Again, simplify. Although an important document in the purchasing cycle, it only needs to contain basic information: the quantity and condition of the merchandise, whether the merchandise tallies with the original purchase order, a record of stock shortages, the recipient's signature and the date of receipt.

Define Your Purchasing Duties

It is all too easy to get bogged down in the day-to-day activities of purchasing. Remind yourself, occasionally, of your areas of responsibility. It helps you to focus on doing a good job.

- **Don't lose sight of your overall goal.** Your responsibility, as a purchasing manager, is to maximize value so that your establishment gets the most for its money. No more, no less.

- **The cycle of duties.** Always bear in mind that a purchaser's areas of responsibility cover an entire cycle of activities: identifying the needs of the establishment, planning, sourcing merchandise, purchasing, receiving, storing and issuing.

- **Control.** Effective management and control of the purchasing cycle, with a constant eye on costs, is your number-one duty.

- **Dealing with vendors.** The purchasing department (even if you are a one-man band) is responsible for all external dealings with vendors. The purchaser should be able to handle all vendor-related queries.

- **Avoid taking your purchasing problems onto the "shop floor."** Front-of-house personnel will not appreciate interruptions while they are trying to please customers. Apart from emergencies, keep all purchasing queries for later.

- **High standards.** It is the purchaser's duty to make sure that all merchandise purchased is fit for its purpose and of a consistently high quality. High standards = good value.

Streamline Your Receiving Procedures

This area of purchasing offers a great scope for cost reductions. Unfortunately, it is often neglected. Do so at your peril! Many well-devised purchasing plans fall at this last hurdle. Don't marginalize this important procedure.

- **Check merchandise thoroughly.** Even when you are in a hurry, it is vital to check all received merchandise carefully. It may be your only (and last) chance to identify problems. Most vendors have a time limit written into their contracts for notifying them of discrepancies and shortages.

- **Adopt a "checklist" approach.** The person receiving the merchandise needs to do the following:
  - Verify the supplier
  - Check quality
  - Check quantity
  - Check price (if applicable)
  - Note any discrepancies on the receiving note
  - Sign and date, only when satisfied with the above

- **Follow up any queries.** Contact the vendor (preferably in writing), outlining any shortages, discrepancies or other problems, immediately. Most problems are quickly resolved. But stating your dissatisfaction, in writing, is a wise move. Sometimes queries become wrangles and you can end up with a long, drawn-out dispute on your hands. It's good to have something in writing!

- **Tie up paperwork.** Tedious, but important! The person who receives the goods or a designated member of staff needs to mark all invoices with some form of "Received" stamp, noting the date of receipt and who received the merchandise.

- **Introduce a random audit of your receiving process.** Identify any problem areas before they get out of hand! A basic audit should compare quantity and quality of merchandise delivered with the original purchase order. Carry out a volume or unit count of liquor, wines and beverages. Also, double-check that cases contain the number of bottles stated on the "outer." Finally, check that all documentation has been accurately processed.

Define Your Purchase Specifications - Define Your Standards

As a purchasing manager, it is important to set standards. Decide up front exactly what types of drinks you need to purchase and the conditions under which you will place an order. These are your purchase specifications.

- **Consult fellow members of staff.** Their input is important. Of course you want them on your side, but oftentimes, it is they who know best what will sell (and what won't!).

- **Purchase specifications must reflect the image of your establishment.** Consider your target audience, the standards it demands and the price it is prepared to pay.

• **Keep a written copy.** It represents your establishment's overall purchasing standards and rules. It doesn't have to be a lengthy document; a few bulleted points will do.

• **Purchase specifications should focus on the following areas:** quality, quantity, consistency, reliability of vendors and availability of merchandise.

• **Document your purchase specifications to vendors.** Vendors need to be reminded of the standards you expect from them. Specs are also useful in the event of a dispute.

• **Back up your purchase specification document with an additional product information list.** Tabulate the information in chart format. Include information such as brand, country of origin, alcohol content (where applicable) and, in the case of wines, year and vintage. Use it to jog your memory when writing out purchase orders or placing orders by phone. This type of handy list can also help you spot "substitutes" when you receive the goods!

Reduce Purchasing Costs

The purchasing department is the linchpin when it comes to reducing costs. It is much easier to control costs in this area than anywhere else in the operation. The bottom line is that astute buying techniques offer the best opportunity for a business to increase its overall profits.

- **Monitor market trends.** An upsurge in popularity of a certain beverage can lead to increased competition amongst vendors. Play them off against each other occasionally. Negotiate. You have nothing to lose!

- **Welcome new ideas.** Purchasers should always be on the lookout for new ideas and new ways of reducing costs. Don't close your door to sales representatives. They may genuinely have something of interest to your establishment. Consider their promotional discounts.

- **"Opportunity buys."** Don't rule them out. Take a look at items that may soon be discontinued or overstocked merchandise where a supplier has simply miscalculated demand. You could make big savings.

- **Cooperative purchasing.** Consider "pool" purchasing with other enterprises. It can give you added purchasing power.

- **Change purchase unit size.** Buy drinks in larger volumes. This can trim costs considerably, particularly in the case of liquor purchases where sell-by dates tend to be more generous.

- **Place multiple orders.** Consider buying your full range of drinks from one wholesaler. It may offer you amazing reductions, especially if it's keen to do business with you on a repeat basis.

Legal and Ethical Issues - Avoid Expensive Mistakes

Whether you like it or not, there's no getting away from the fact that almost every aspect of purchasing has certain legal or ethical implications. Daunting? It shouldn't be. All you need is a very basic grasp of those areas of contract and commercial law that affect your company. A little understanding of the consequences of your actions as a buyer will go a long way. It will help you protect your company's interests.

- **Acquire a few basics.** Read a beginner's guide on the subject of contract law or search the Internet for information.

- **Know your limitations.** A basic grasp of the risks will enable you to recognize problems that require specialized legal advice or intervention. If in doubt, consult the experts. You have done what is required of you: you have identified the problem.

- **Contracts.** Ask a legal professional to draft all written company contracts. No amount of legal "reading around" will equip you with the knowledge to draw up a bona fide contract. Bear in mind, however, that contracts don't have to be written.

- **Familiarize yourself with all your suppliers' contracts.** Content can differ considerably.

- **Liquor, wine and beverage descriptions.** A veritable legal minefield - if you get it wrong. Every detail of the drinks list must be 100-percent accurate. If selling substitutes, state so clearly. Keep your guests informed.

- **Create a network of trust with your vendors.**
  This is particularly important in the liquor and
  beverages industry where, unfortunately, unethical
  practices are commonplace.

- **Conform to ISM standards.** Every company
  purchaser should abide by the ethical credo of the
  "Institute for Supply Management." It advocates:
  "Loyalty to this company; Justice to those with
  whom you deal; Faith in your profession." For
  more information, visit www.ism.ws or call
  800-888-6276.

CHAPTER FOUR

INVENTORY CONTROL

General Inventory Procedures

Minor overall changes can result in major cost reductions. Take a fresh look at your existing inventory system. In every establishment, there is general room for improvement. For minimum effort, you can get maximum value out of your stock.

- **Timing.** Move all drinks to a designated storage area as soon as they arrive. Don't let stock hang around. Drinks (and wine especially) need to be stored in an ambient environment, or their quality can deteriorate rapidly - and so can your profits! Also, unattended drinks, languishing in receiving areas, present a great temptation. Liquor is high on any thief's hit list.

- **Faulty goods.** When receiving merchandise, look out for cracked and chipped bottles, mislabeled boxes, outdated or cloudy beer, correct type and vintage of wine, raised corks, leaking and weeping bottles, damaged labels and wrong-size bottles. Contact the supplier immediately about any discrepancies.

- **Storage area.** Your storage area must be fit for its purpose. Poor storage conditions can result in poor quality, breakage and escalating costs.

- **Security.** Basic, but obvious. A good security system removes temptation and reduces the risk of external break-ins.

- **Rotate stock.** First in, first out. This is important and avoids wastage, overstocking and running out. Pay special attention to beers: their shelf-life is limited. Most beverages, also, have no longer than a month before the sell-by date.

- **Control.** Large or small, every drinks outlet needs some form of control procedure. Track your products from the moment they arrive at your premises to when they are sold. While this doesn't have to be complicated, the key to any good control system is to make sure that all the liquors, wines and beverages are located in the right place at the right time and are being rotated properly.

Make the Most of Your Storage Areas

Where and how you store your liquor, wines and beverages can make a big difference in turnover and profits. Once you have taken delivery, treat your inventory with respect - it has the potential to make or break your business.

- **Location.** Define storage areas. Are you using the most convenient areas for storage? Rethink. Centrally located storerooms and walk-in coolers make ideal storage areas. Easy access saves time and money.

- **Other storage areas.** "Storage" means more than an area for dumping received goods! Storage locations include shelves, workstations, reach-in refrigerators and behind the bar. Keep all these areas accessible and clutter-free. It speeds up your operation and reduces breakage.

- **High-value wines.** Consider separate cellaring for prestige wines, somewhere away from the busy "shop floor" environment. As turnover of such wines is slower, accessibility is not top priority. More important is security and perfect storage conditions (even vibrations can affect the quality of good wines!).

- **Extra security.** All drinks should be stored in a secure area. Organize the layout of storage areas to offer maximum security for liquor and high-value wines. Only personnel who need keys should have them.

- **Quantity.** Drinks can be stored in bulk in the main storage area. Drinks in general storage areas, such as behind the bar, are better stored in the units or quantities in which they are sold.

- **Environment.** Know your product and store it accordingly. Maintain proper temperatures, humidity and ventilation. Wine is particularly sensitive to environmental influences. It can easily absorb odors from nearby food storage areas. Poor storage practices can quickly reduce the quality of stored inventory - and nothing affects profits like quality!

Track Inventory · Track Costs

In order to control inventory, you need to know exactly what stock you have/had and where it is or when you sold it (known in the trade as "cradle-to-grave" accounting). To operate a cost-effective tracking procedure, it is crucial that you document all liquor, wines and beverages as they progress through the inventory cycle. Choose whatever tracking method works best for your establishment, but don't think you can do without some form of system. You can't. On a positive note, however, developing such a system is one of the best ways of keeping a tight rein on expenditure. Follow this six-step guideline and you shouldn't go wrong! There are several cheap, off-the-shelf forms that you can use to help you with your record keeping.

- **Step 1: Purchase order.** The purchase order is the first form in the cycle. It provides a detailed record of every item purchased.

- **Step 2: Perpetual inventory.** This second form tracks the movement of liquor, wines and beverages from the storeroom to various locations within the establishment. It also tracks each product's turnover rate. The perpetual inventory is also used for accounting purposes.

- **Step 3: Requisition form.** This records the actual transfer of inventory from the storeroom to a specific location within the operation. This form is also used to record breakage.

- **Step 4: Bar par form.** This records the quantity of each brand of liquor, wine or beverage currently stocked behind the bar.

- **Step 5: Depletion allowance form.** This form is used to track the amount of spillage and wastage and to record any complimentary drinks.

- **Step 6: Physical inventory form.** Used primarily when completing end-of-period accounts, it records the result of physical stock audits.

Monthly and Annual Inventory Control

Daily inventory control is the first, essential step towards keeping costs in check. In fact, no business can function without daily records. But, look ahead. To maximize control of overall costs, establish sound monthly and annual inventory procedures. Drain every dime out of your liquor, wine and beverage inventory - long-term!

- **Monthly inventory.** Month-end figures are crucial for determining the financial success of your operation. Devise a simple monthly inventory sheet and use it, without fail.

- **Physical count.** Carry out a monthly physical bottle count. Check totals against the perpetual inventory figures.

- **The "Cyclops."** This handheld scanner reads the Universal Pricing Code (UPC). It can really speed up the monthly stock check! For information about bar-code scanners, see the following links:

  Symbol
  www.symbol.com

  Barcode Man
  www.barcodeman.com

- **Weighing scale.** Use a precision liquor-weighing scale. These devices are extremely fast and easy to use. They can calculate to within 1/40 of a fluid ounce.

- **Annual inventory.** Use annual inventory figures to review overall costs. For example, now is the time to consider price increases or to discontinue lines that are no longer cost-effective.

- **Resolve queries.** Merely recording monthly and annual inventory figures is not enough. Resolve any discrepancies immediately. It all adds up!

Inventory Levels Affect Cash Flow

The aim is to maintain that fine balance between running out and holding too much stock. Get it wrong, and you'll find that your working capital isn't working for you! Remember, the larger your inventory, the more difficult it is to control.

- **Keep inventory at a minimum level.** But not so low that you risk running out. Recommended inventory for high-turnover brands is approximately one to two weeks' worth of stock.

- **Jump in with special promotions.** If you think you've miscalculated and overstocked, shift the inventory sooner rather than later, while it still has high value.

- **Get to know the drinking patterns of your regular patrons.** This information helps you calculate the bar pars or minimum inventory levels for each bar and the main stockroom.

- **The perpetual inventory is a valuable tool.**
  Keeping tabs on the flow of liquor, wines and
  beverages through your operation is probably the
  best way of knowing where to pitch inventory
  levels. Monitor stock daily.

- **Weekly deliveries.** In the drinks industry, this is
  the norm. Work your inventory levels around these
  weekly deliveries and avoid the cardinal sin of
  running out.

Manage Your Stock Wisely and Maximize Profits

Your challenge, in a nutshell, is to order liquor, wine
and other beverages in the right size and quantity
and at the right time and price.

- **Inventory deliveries - timing.** Schedule well
  liquor, beer and house wine deliveries for the same
  day each week, ideally a couple days after you
  place the order.

- **Well liquor quantities.** Order items with a short
  turnover rate, such as well liquor, in bulk. Well
  liquor moves fast, offering you a great opportunity
  to boost cash flow. Take advantage of case
  discounts. Also, consider larger 1.75-liter bottles
  instead of the usual 1-liter bottles if you think
  your turnover warrants it. There are big savings to
  be made in this area. Use larger bottles for special
  promotions.

- **Beer is different.** In order to sell beer at its
  freshest, arrange for deliveries on a weekly basis,
  or daily, if your establishment has the capacity to
  cope with the extra workload. Little and often is

better when it comes to maximizing on beer profits.

- **Wine.** Order house wine weekly, other wine bottles by the case once a month. Only buy special vintage wines once or twice a year. Take a specialist's advice before stocking up on expensive wines. They can cost you dearly.

- **Liquor and liqueurs.** The following is a useful guideline: If it takes less than five weeks to turn a product, order by the case. If it takes longer than five weeks to sell a particular brand of spirits, order by the liter.

Reduce Inventory Pilferage

Don't leave stock security to chance. Any slackness in this area can seriously dent profits. Your central storeroom may well be as secure as a vault, but this isn't good enough. Tight security is essential in all locations where inventory is stored - from reception to behind the bar. Design a security system that ensures that all liquor, wines and beverages stay in their correct location throughout the operation. The following security techniques will help reduce pilferage:

- **Storeroom keys.** Change locks and combinations regularly. Insist that all keys remain on the premises at all times.

- **Roll-down screens and lockable cabinets.** Keep high-value inventory inaccessible to cleaning staff and other employees when the bar is closed.

- **Limit access.** Only key members of staff, such as management, receiving and storage personnel, should be allowed to enter the storeroom. It is also a good idea to limit the issuing of inventory to specific, set times.

- **Lockable refrigerators and walk-in coolers.** All storage areas should be completely lockable. Alternatively, have at least one lockable shelf for the highest-value inventory.

- **Bar stock security.** Danger zone! Keep the quantity of liquor and beverages stored behind the bar to a workable minimum.

- **Investigate state-of-the-art locking devices.** They may prove a sound long-term investment. Systems that involve combinations, codes, PINs and swipe cards are becoming increasingly popular.

Reduce Costs · Streamline Issuing Procedures

Revise your existing issuing procedures. You'll be surprised at how much cost trimming you can achieve in this area. Issuing procedures are particularly vulnerable to employee theft and wastage. Establish a simple issuing procedure that focuses on reducing costs. Keep the following basic records:

- **End of shift.** Bartenders need to record the name of each liquor, wine and beverage emptied during their shifts. They should also note the number of empty bottles and the size of the bottles. Make bartenders responsible for this activity. They will feel accountable.

- **Manager authorization.** Managers should check empty bottles against the beverage requisition form at the end of each shift. It is much easier and more cost-effective for resolving any problems immediately than letting minor queries develop into major problems at a later date.

- **Issuing replacement stock.** Either the manager or the bartender is the best person to return empty bottles and the completed requisition form to the storeroom. The person replacing the empties should check all the information on the requisition and issue replacements, bottle for bottle.

- **Breakage.** It is important to account for breakage each time the requisition form is completed. Not only does it give you tighter control over cash flow, it also helps identify potential (and costly) problem areas - sooner rather than later.

- **Daily cost keeping.** Calculate, on a daily basis, the total cost of inventory issued. This should be viewed as a separate management or administrative function. It provides an essential "cross-check."

- **Computerized issuing.** A manual issuing procedure works well in many small establishments. But, if you have the resources, opt for a computerized system. It will quickly repay your investment. For information about computerized solutions, contact:

ICE
www.horizons.bc.ca/ice/index.html
604-589-8130

Scannabar
www.liquorinventory.com 800-666-0736

Inventory Valuation Made Easy

Daunted by the pros and cons of the various accounting procedures used in today's liquor, wine and beverage industry? No need. Choose the approach that best meets the requirements of your establishment. Keep it simple. The following methods are tried and tested. They are also known for their ability to control cash flow and to reduce overall costs.

- **FIFO (first in, first out).** This means that items in storage are valued at the level of the most-recently purchased items. FIFO helps maximize profits by extending inventory value, particularly when inflation is high. A word of warning, though: Make sure that all profits are accurately recorded and that all drinks are rotated on a strictly first-in, first-out basis.

- **LIFO (last in, first out).** Here, the most-recent items are recorded as the first ones used. This method is useful when prices are rising, fast. Rotate stock on a FIFO basis, but make sure that the value of the inventory reflects the oldest purchase prices. If your product valuation is keenly affected by inflation, use LIFO!

- **Actual Method.** With the Actual Method, the inventory is valued at actual cost. It's a bit time consuming, unless you have a computerized system - even then, the Actual Method is probably not the best choice for reducing costs.

- **Last Price Method.** Similar to FIFO, this is one of the most commonly used accounting procedures used in the beverage industry today. It involves using the last purchase price to extend inventory value.

- **Computerized packages.** Whatever your choice of method, a good-off-the-shelf package for calculating inventory values is a must.

Bar Inventory

Wastage, spillage, employee theft, oversights and inefficiency are most likely to occur in the working environment of a busy bar. Improved management of bar inventory can make a big impact on profits. Even one bottle of liquor represents a substantial profit - or loss. Introduce a few changes behind the bar. Small adjustments can make a big difference!

- **Security-mark bottles.** Security-mark every bottle of liquor destined for the bar when it is received into the storeroom. This identifying mark, stamp or nonremovable label (placed on the bottom or side of the bottle) proves that the bottle belongs to your operation. If you are using a computer-controlled inventory system, consider using a bar-coded label for better inventory control.

- **Unauthorized sales.** Empty bottles returned without a mark indicate that bar staff may possibly be serving liquor from unauthorized bottles. It is not unknown for employees to bring in their own bottles in the hope of making a fast buck!

- **Control cards.** All inventory requisitioned by the bar must be recorded in the perpetual inventory, usually by computer. A backup card system can act as an invaluable "double check." Don't make it complicated. All you need is a date and signature against the item.

- **Bin cards.** Bin cards give you extra control over high-value items. Fix small index cards (known in the trade as bin cards) to the shelves where such items are located. Keep a careful eye on the running totals.

- **Backup liquor.** Even on a typical busy night, one bottle of premium liquor and two to six bottles of well liquor is sufficient backup.

- **Accurate records.** Distinguish clearly between unopened and opened bottles when valuing inventory. Opened bottles should be measured to the nearest tenth of a bottle, using dipsticks or by weight.

Standardization of all liquid and beverage portions is critical.

CHAPTER FIVE

PORTION CONTROL

Portion Standardization - Putting It into Practice

Behind a busy bar, it just isn't realistic to expect a bartender to stop and consult a lengthy list of standard portion requirements every time a customer places an order! Yet, standardization of all liquor, wine and beverage portions is critical. Here are a few shortcuts.

- **Know your establishment's regular clientele.** Devise a simple chart of the most popular drinks requested on a regular basis. A few clear, bulleted instructions are all you'll need most of the time. This list will probably cover around 90 percent of orders. It should provide a quick point of reference for busy bartenders. In the interests of credibility, keep it out of customer sight.

- **The full guidelines.** To cover all other eventualities, keep a detailed guideline to portion standardization easily accessible behind the bar. Make sure that the information is simple to follow and regularly updated.

- **Educate employees.** Portion errors caused by ignorance can ruin your operation, fast. You can also lose out big-time when bartenders are tired, bored or under pressure. They're easy to spot: they will often take shortcuts, such as lining up glasses and pouring straight across the top without pausing. Eliminate this type of activity.

- **Keep an eye on "mixer" portions.** Strict portion standardization should apply equally to the non-alcoholic content of all "mixed" drinks. Bartenders need to be reminded of the fact that all portions add up - alcoholic and nonalcoholic alike.

- **Consistency.** A vital factor in achieving portion standardization. Make sure that all drinks are poured in a consistent fashion. This helps ensure accurate portion control as well as consistency of quality.

Precision Portioning Boosts Profits

So much hinges on portion control! If portion size fluctuates, so will profit margins. For example, if a bartender overpours the high-value of a drink by as little as half an ounce on a regular basis, the cost of that drink can escalate by as much as six to ten percent. Multiply this wastage over a period of time and the results can be devastating. It is, therefore, essential to implement an effective strategy for portion control, or profits will suffer. The following is a summary of the main pros and cons of methods used for portion control in the drinks industry.

- **Free-pouring.** The bartender has to rely on a spout attached to the bottle to control the rate of flow. Although the free-pouring method is fast and easy, it has obvious shortcomings when it comes to cost control.

- **Handheld portioning.** This involves pouring the liquor into a shot glass or "jigger" - a popular method that is reasonably reliable and cost-effective.

- **Bottle-attached controls.** Better than free-pouring and handheld measuring, these devices can deliver with impressive accuracy.

- **Liquor Control Systems (LCS).** The use of technologically advanced portion-control systems is becoming increasingly commonplace in today's drinks industry. LCSs are particularly effective at controlling liquor costs. They can also virtually eliminate employee theft. LCSs are marketed on the basis of a typical return on investment within twelve months. The following suppliers offer LCSs:

  Berg Company
  www.berg-controls.com 608-221-4281

  AzBar
  www.azbaramerica.com 214-361-2422

  Bristol BM
  www.bristolnf.com/liquor.htm 709-722-6669

Control Portions and Meet Customer Expectations

Inadequate portion control can lead to unforeseen customer care problems - and customer dissatisfaction is only one of them! Incorrect portioning can also have costly legal implications. Consider the following:

- **Portion inconsistency is a major source of customer complaint**. If drink portions are strictly controlled, guests will be served the same drink every time, no matter which bartender pours it. The customer is satisfied.

- **Get ratios right.** Customers will complain (and quite rightly so) if drinks are mixed in the wrong proportions. Standard recipes must comply with fixed portions for each ingredient. Mistakes can cost you more than the price of an extra portion; they can cost you a regular customer.

- **Dram Shop Acts.** Many states have passed legislation imposing third-party liability on liquor servers and licensees who cannot control the effects of customer intoxication. Proprietors can be held responsible (under certain circumstances) for the actions of customers who consume excessive amounts of alcohol. Incorrect portioning is frequently to blame. In the worst cases, this can result in bankruptcy for the liquor supplier. For more resources, visit: www.tf.org/tf/alcohol/ariv/dram4.html.

- **Beware of serving doubles.** A double is more than twice as potent as a single. This is because the ratio of spirit to mixer is inverted. Doubles are good for profit, but serve them with caution.

Monitor Portions Effectively

It is the obligation of every beverage manager to meet the rigorous standards for portion control as defined by the drinks industry. Once standards have been established, however, they need to be monitored continuously. Herein lies the challenge for the busy bar manager:

- **Be realistic.** Strike a balance between the time and effort required to develop a portion-monitoring system and its effectiveness in practice.

- **Be specific at the purchasing stage.** State size, weight and count (and any other details that are specifically related to portion control) in sufficient detail to guide suppliers and receiving personnel.

- **Standard recipes**. Always stick to the correct formulas for the proportions of all drinks. Do not improvise.

- **Enforce the serving of standard portions behind the bar.** Use pouring methods that are effectively self-monitoring.

- **Introduce monitoring tools.** These need to be the types of devices that will actually help, rather than hinder, busy bartenders. Automated beverage dispensers are a good idea.

- **Monitor the cost of portions as well as the size.** Work out the cost of preparing (as well as the cost of the ingredients) for one drink. It is all too easy to assume that if the size is right, so is the cost. The results could be interesting! Review this aspect of portion control on a regular basis. It is a lucrative area for reducing costs.

Improve Portion Control in the Restaurant

How drinks are served at the table can have a major impact upon an establishment's overall costs and profits. Portion control is a far more complex issue in a restaurant environment. Here, the serving of drinks is only one aspect of the whole dining experience. Other factors have to be considered, such as the relationship between server and diner.

- **The customer is always right.** Guest satisfaction should lead the way to portion control. This approach might at first seem contradictory, but it will ultimately prove a more effective way in which to control drink portions.

- **Don't underpour.** Again, it may seem somewhat contradictory, but short measures invariably lead to customer dissatisfaction and the demand for overcompensation.

- **Drink menus.** Make sure that menus on both the bar and tables specify the exact contents of each drink. This information applies not only to the ingredients but also to the alcohol/nonalcohol ounce content. Customers like to know exactly what they're drinking - and in what volume.

- **Wine and spirit glasses.** Attractive drinking glasses considerably enhance diner enjoyment and result in the impulse ordering of additional portions.

- **Standardize drink portions** - unobtrusively! Servers must be trained to fill glasses to just the right level - no more, no less. They should also, at the same time, make the procedure appear effortless.

- **Mixed drinks.** Drinks waiters in the restaurant need to apply the same rigid portion controls as bar staff. It is easy to overpour in a dining environment.

- **Wine portions.** Serve wine in both a "regular" and a "large" wineglass. If the customer doesn't stipulate a preference, you are not breaking the law by defaulting to "large," merely boosting profits.

Reduce Wastage · Reduce Portion Costs

A certain amount of wastage is inevitable in any drinks outlet. The key, however, is to keep it to a minimum. Introduce a few practical measures that can really make a difference.

- **Inter-bar transfer.** Discourage this activity as much as possible. Only move bottles around the establishment if it is absolutely necessary. Ideally, stock should be moved only twice; from reception to storeroom and from storeroom to bar.

- **Cleanliness.** Make sure that all draft beer lines are scrupulously clean and functioning at optimum capacity. If in doubt, ask the brewery that supplied you the beer to carry out regular maintenance checks.

- **Don't skimp on the "pulling through" of draft beers.** This applies to the first portion of beer from a new barrel. It is crucial to "waste" a complete portion in order to maintain quality standards. To do otherwise is false economy.

- **Complimentary drinks.** Remind bar staff to record complimentary drinks at all times. Even one unrecorded portion per shift can have a long-term impact on profits.

- **Bar layout.** Careful planning is required to allow bartenders maximum freedom of movement. Cramped serving conditions can result in excessive spillage and wasted portions.

- **Spoilage.** Don't overlook the portions of "add on" ingredients, such as ice cream, that are stored in open containers behind the bar. Only keep sufficient stock to fill the orders for one shift. Leftovers cannot be reused.

Mixed Drinks - Get the Proportions Right!

Correct portioning is a vital aspect, not only of achieving customer satisfaction, but also of maintaining profitability and reducing costs behind the bar. Guests will notice immediately if drinks lack "balance." In addition, beware: You could be violating beverage laws if you serve drinks in the incorrect proportions!

- **Fixed portions.** Establish serving portions for each main type of mixed drink served in your establishment. Stick to these predetermined portions at all times.

- **Portioning guidelines.** Bartenders must be given clear instructions regarding the exact composition of each mixed drink. This applies to all types of drink, from highballs to liqueur coffees.

- **Optics.** Don't risk getting the proportions wrong - use an optic to dispense the alcoholic component of mixed drinks.

- **"Baby" bottles.** Miniature bottles of nonalcoholic

ingredients are easier to use and more accurate than draft "mixers."

- **Don't ignore the trimmings.** Add-ons, such as ice, lemon slices and cream, also need to be served in correct-size portions.

- **Computerized recipe calculators.** Install off-the-shelf or online recipe management software that calculates the correct proportions for standard mixed drinks. A great time-saver, it will also reduce error margins significantly. Some supplier links:

  Ace Bartender
  www.acebartender.com

  Bar Bug
  www.barbug.com

  Bar Fliers
  www.barfliers.com

Serve Drinks in the Correct Glassware

Using the correct glassware is one of the best ways of improving portion control. Serve drinks in the appropriate glass, and you'll soon notice the difference! It is also a simple yet effective way of reducing costs and boosting profits.

- **Range of glassware.** Invest in a range of the most-common-sized glassware, such as six- to-eight-ounce rock glasses, nine-to-ten-ounce highball, eleven- to-fourteen-ounce bucket glasses and six-to- fourteen-ounce snifters. These high-usage glasses will help to ensure that drinks are served in the correct portions.

- **Individuality.** Don't be afraid to choose glassware that reflects the style of your establishment. For example, if you sell mainly draft beer, you will need to stock up on traditional pint and half-pint glasses - good for the image but also essential for portion control.

- **Present premium cocktails in expensive-looking glassware.** Boost sales in this high-profit sector of the drinks' market. Sophisticated cocktail glasses will practically market the drinks for you.

- **Marked glasses.** Don't shy away from stocking up on glasses marked with the required standard liquor levels. Customers, in general, prefer their drinks served in these types of glasses. They know they are not being "short measured." You also benefit from more accurate portion control.

Pouring Beers and Ales in the Correct Portions

Portion control of beers and ales can present quite a challenge compared with serving almost any other beverage. Beer, brewed and fermented from cereal grains, and ale, a similar product but with a higher hop content, are complex drinks that demand extra-special care and attention.

- **Don't overstock.** Beers and ales are highly perishable. Quality will quickly deteriorate, especially in the case of draft beer. Even canned and bottled beers can have "pull dates" or sell-by dates as short as a couple of weeks.

- **Rotate stock.** Stock rotation is extremely important with beers and ales. Monitor all dates on draft, bottled and canned beers, both in the storeroom and behind the bar.

- **Quality.** Apart from monitoring consistent freshness, make sure that beer is served cold, at approximately 40° F. Customers will soon complain if the temperature is wrong.

- **Draw or pour beer properly.** The skilled bartender must acquire the correct technique for pouring beer, whether draft or from a bottle or can. Regular spillage down the side of the glass can reduce profits dramatically.

- **Beer "head."** Control the size of the "head" you put on each glass by holding the glass at a slight angle at the beginning of the draw. Too sharp an angle will result in excess foam and portion wastage.

Alcoholic Beverages and the Law - Strict Portion Control

All establishments, including bars, taverns, restaurants, banquet venues and nightclubs - in fact, any outlet that sells beverages containing ethyl alcohol - must comply with strict government alcohol regulations. Federal inspectors demand total compliance.

- **Stock and serve standard portions only.** Portion control means more than just cost control. It has serious legal implications.

- **Know the rules.** You have no option but to familiarize yourself with government legislation regarding the selling and serving of alcoholic drinks. Pay special attention to the "Dram Shop Laws." These acts stipulate that the liquor vendor is liable for the actions of intoxicated guests. Understand your obligations.

- **Alert bar staff.** Train employees to serve alcoholic beverages in the correct portions. They should also be able to spot the early signs of customer intoxication. If in doubt, bartenders should refuse to serve anyone who is visibly intoxicated. Management should always support their decisions.

- **Clear labeling.** The federal government has fixed standards for identifying all types of distilled spirits, wines and malt beverages. Stick to these standards. Make sure that all alcoholic products sold in your establishment are clearly labeled with the correct alcohol content and point of origin.

CHAPTER SIX

THEFT

Insider Theft

This is an alarming fact: most types of beverage operations lose a crippling percentage of profits through insider theft. The vast majority of employees in the beverage industry are honest and hardworking; it is the small minority of staff that can ruin your business through dishonesty. Insider theft can often escalate if there are weaknesses in the following general areas of the operation:

- **Lack of supervision.** Theft from behind the bar, storeroom or storage areas is a major problem. Curb losses by increasing supervision, either in person or by means of strategically positioned security cameras.

- **Proprietor attitude.** Don't make matters worse by treating all employees with suspicion. Get the honest staff on your side.

- **Weak management.** Unfortunately, some beverage managers compound the issue of insider theft by turning a "blind eye" and simply increasing prices to cover "shrinkage." Owners need to question unwarranted price rises.

- **Pouring costs (PC).** A common danger area. These costs need to be carefully monitored, especially in relation to bartender productivity.

- **Inventory records.** This is one of the easiest areas for dishonest employees to "fiddle the books." Tighten up your record keeping. Never leave inventory control to one person. Double-check.

- **End-of-shift cash count.** Another prime target area for insider theft. Never let a bartender reconcile the cash in the register at the end of his or her shift.

Bartender Theft - Top-Ten Common Ploys

Controlling theft behind the majority of bars is no mean task; eliminating it altogether is virtually impossible. Temptation is a fine thing, and unfortunately, the opportunity for bartender theft is overwhelming. However, in the interests of long-term survival, you have no choice but to tackle the problem head on. Be wary of the following top-ten common ploys:

- **Open theft.** A bartender pours a drink, doesn't ring the cash register and puts the cash in a "holding" place, such as the tip jar.

- **Overcharging.** Bartender pockets the difference. A variation is to charge regular prices but ring up "Happy Hour" prices and, again, pocket the difference.

- **Ringing "00" on the cash register.** The bartender simply steals the value of the drink.

- **Overpouring.** Bartender hopes to get a heavy tip.

- **Underpouring.** Bartender keeps a mental note of the number of half measures poured throughout the evening and then thieves the equivalent value in drinks, gives them away or drinks them him-or herself.

- **Rounds of drinks.** Bartender rings up for a "round" rather than separate items. It makes it easier to inflate the overall price of a round of drinks, particularly if guests are unfamiliar with individual prices.

- **Shortchanging.** Common variations include: counting aloud while handing the customer less money, distracting the customer by sliding the change along the bar, and giving change for lower-denomination bills (while keeping the difference).

- **"Soft" inventory.** Bartender neglects to charge for the mixer component of a drink.

- **Substitution - bringing in own liquor.** This is often done with vodka because it is odorless and looks like water. Dilution is another similar ploy.

- **Padding the tab.** The bartender pencils in an inflated total and later erases it, replacing it with the correct total. Warning! Ban pencils from behind the bar.

Less Common (But Equally Damaging) Employee Theft

The more experienced the dishonest employee, the better equipped he or she is to manipulate the system. Thieving members of staff are quick to detect exactly how much an owner really understands about the business. In the beverage industry, take nothing for granted. Alert yourself to the following, somewhat extreme, possibilities.

- **Bartender brings in counterfeit money.** Fraudsters tend to reserve such bills specifically for passing trade and tourists.

- **Reusing closed tabs.** The bartender appears to ring up the drink price but, in actual fact, only halfway enters the tab into the register. He or she then hits "0" to give the impression of ringing it in.

- **Cash register tape.** The bartender brings in his or her own cash register tape, prepared on a leased cash register that is identical to the one in the workplace. Total takings can be "adjusted" according to the greed of the thief. Warning! Don't let bartenders "Z" tapes from their own shifts.

- **Over-ringing.** When the customer isn't looking, the thief over-rings an amount on the tab and then re-rings the tab for less than the amount charged.

- **"Paid outs."** The bartender claims that the money was refunded for various reasons, such as faulty cigarette machines.

- **Charge cards.** Old, manual, slide-style machines are particularly vulnerable. The thief may place a "block" in between the top copy and the remaining copies and later alter the total.

- **Jigger substitution.** The bartender brings in his own shot glass that looks identical to the official jigger but is actually smaller. Several short measures over a shift add up.

- **Changing shifts.** It is easy for the thief to make, serve and collect several drinks during a busy "hand-over" period.

- **Deliberate mistakes.** Drinks are then returned and resold or given to a friend.

- **Breaking empty bottles and pretending they were full.** Full bottles are then requisitioned to replace the "broken" empty bottles.

- **Substituting water in the drip tray.** The bartender pretends he or she had to waste a pint to clear the lines and then pockets the difference.

Explore the Underlying "Excuses" for Theft

Take a step back and explore why thieving is rife in the beverage industry. Your motives may not be entirely altruistic for doing so, but the fact remains - if you're trying to reduce costs, you need to know what you're up against. An informed manager is in a much stronger position to take steps to control and reduce "wastage" due to theft.

- **Fear.** Dishonest employees are governed by the fear of detection. The prospect of being fired without a reference is a major deterrent. If you need to use this threat, do so without hesitation.

- **Rationalizing theft.** Employees contemplating theft will first have to "justify" the risks to themselves. They will have to weigh the possibility of getting caught compared with the potential gains. Don't put temptation in their way. Keep high-value inventory under lock and key.

- **The importance of tips.** Tips make up a significant part of any bartender's pay. Dishonest employees in financial difficulty have a tendency to abuse the tipping system before they turn their attentions to the rest of the establishment. The tips jar makes exceptionally easy pickings.

- **Greed.** Some thieves simply enjoy the challenge of "getting one over" on management. They're bored and looking for excitement.

- **Resentment.** Sometimes staff resent taking orders and believe, for whatever reason, that they're being "picked on." In the interests of the overall success of the operation, managers must appear, at all times, to be acting fairly and reasonably.

Introduce Theft-Reduction Procedures That Are Easy to Enforce

Theft reduction policies and procedures are no good unless they are strictly enforced. Employees must be made clearly aware of the dire consequences of flouting house rules. There can be no gray areas. New members of staff should be asked to sign a confirmation that they have read the rules and fully understand the implications.

- **Prohibit bartenders from totaling the cash at the end of their shifts.** This policy also protects honest bar staff.

- **Prohibit bartenders from both on- and off-duty drinking.** Off-duty drinking leads to fellow bar staff overpouring, giving away free drinks or undercharging.

- **Prohibit bartenders from taking part in physical inventory counts.** Ideally this should be a management-only function.

- **Bartenders should not be involved in ordering, receiving or issuing inventory.** Again, this should be a management-only function.

- **Security.** Enforce security procedures for all liquor, wine, beer, spirits and any other high-value inventory. Also, only key personnel should have access to the storeroom.

- **Require bartenders to record post-shift bar par readings**. This refers to the number of bottles behind the bar at any given time. Bartenders should take a bar par reading at the end of the night shift.

- **Prohibit bartenders from recording more than one transaction per drink ticket.** If bartenders are allowed to use a "running" ticket, they can easily neglect to record all the drinks they have actually sold.

- **Enforce voiding procedures.** Bartenders should request managerial approval before continuing with a void.

Reduce Opportunities for Thieving

In reality it is almost impossible to eliminate theft in the beverage industry. However, a knowledge of the numerous, cunning scams used by bartenders and other members of staff to steal from their employers is a big step in the right direction. Have you thought of the following?

- **Tip jar.** Positioning cash jars too close to the cash register is asking for trouble. It's far too easy for bartenders to slip stolen cash from the register into the jar, a temporary hiding place. Also, in some establishments the tip jar is used to get change for the register. Bad move. Thieves can easily exchange tip cash for larger denominations from the cash drawer during this type of transaction.

- **Time cards.** Time clock fraud is quite a common occurrence. Time is money, so it's a good idea to get the manager on duty to sign employees' time cards at the end of each shift.

- **No sale.** Nip this one in the bud. Watch out for bartenders who sell a drink and then ring up "no sale." The easiest way to restrict this practice is to have a security feature added to the "no sale" button. Another suggestion is to insist that bartenders ring in the sale before serving the drink.

- **Test a bartender's honesty.** Sneaky, but effective! Slip an extra $10 or $20 bill into the opening bank. Ask bartenders to verify the amount of money in the register's opening bank and see whether they inform you of the planted "over."

Identify and Prevent Bookkeeper Theft

Accounting (bookkeeping) theft is a major concern within the beverage industry. From falsifying daily inventory records to complicated auditing abuse, this area of theft is often the most difficult to detect. Sometimes, it is the managers themselves who are behind the scams. Owners need to be aware of the following possibilities:

- **Sales records** - falsifying daily sales records and stealing the difference between recorded and actual cash received.

- **Inflating overtime** - adding overtime or extra hours to payroll records in order to increase wages.

- **Discounts** - recording higher-than-actual discounts when reimbursement checks from credit card companies are deposited.

- **Forging signatures** - making checks payable to oneself, then forging signatures or using signed blank checks, then destroying paid checks returned from the bank.

- **Falsifying bank statement reconciliations** - overrecording deposits that have not been recorded, underrecording outstanding checks or even deliberately miscalculating reconciliation worksheets with the intention of covering cash shortages.

- **Overpaying suppliers' invoices** - then converting the suppliers' refund check for personal use.

- **Resubmitting invoices** - duplicating requests for payment and splitting the difference with dishonest suppliers.

- **Dummy companies** - setting up "dummy" companies and using them to submit invoices for payment.

- **"Padding" the payroll** - issuing checks for fictitious members of staff or employees who no longer work for the company.

Minimize Inventory Theft

This is no mean task in the beverage industry! But you can take damage-limitation measures. Strict control of inventory procedures throughout the operation can have a major impact upon reducing costs through unnecessary "wastage." Implement the following tried and proven procedures.

- **Bartenders should not take part in physical inventory procedures.** It gives dishonest employees the perfect opportunity to alter the records to offset previous theft. Taking the bar's physical inventory should be a management function.

- **Bartenders should not take part in purchasing, ordering, receiving or issuing liquor.** These, also, should be managerial functions.

- **Secure inventory.** Lock all liquor, wine, beer and high-value inventory in a secure storeroom or storage area. Limit access to key personnel.

- **Banquet or "function" bartenders should not be allowed behind the main bar.** Otherwise, it would be easy for banquet bartenders to move liquor to the bar and then steal it later on.

- **Control inventory in transit from store to bar.** The scope is immense here for the dishonest bartender. It has even been known for full bottles of liquor to find their way into outside trash cans, to be recovered later by the thief.

- **Computerized inventory control.** Manual inventory record keeping is wide open to abuse. The best way of reducing costs incurred through inventory theft is to install a computerized perpetual inventory system. Investigate computerized solutions, including:

  Scannabar
  www.liquorinventory.com 800-666-0736

  Berg Company
  www.berg-controls.com 608-221-4281

Manager Theft - The Danger Areas

Beverage managers are in powerful positions; they are trusted. A dishonest manager can easily conceal fraudulent activities until it is too late to rescue the business. The scope for dishonesty amongst middle management, in particular, should never be underestimated. No one is in a better situation to defraud the operation than a thieving middle manager. Beware of the following examples of manager theft:

- **Stealing cash receipts and inventory.** In most beverage operations, managers are responsible for removing cash from the register at the end of each shift and preparing the opening banks and daily deposits. A dishonest manager could easily take a premature "Z" reading, or steal cash receipts and claim that the bartender's cash draw was short.

- **Collusion.** "Team work" involving thieving bartenders and managers is unfortunately all too common in the beverage industry.

- **Inventory abuse.** A manager is in the ideal position to offset previous theft without raising suspicion, by simply altering the records and per-petuating fraud.

- **Defrauding bank deposit funds.** An interesting solution to the problem is for the owner to allocate this particular task to junior members of staff on a rotational basis. The secret is not to give any one person overall responsibility for depositing cash in the establishment's bank account.

- **"Spotters."** If you suspect theft by management, employ a professional "spotter" or "mystery shopping service" to scrutinize your operation. Spotters, in the beverage trade, will have an in-depth knowledge of beverage prices, procedures and policies. They will "infiltrate" your establish-ment, as plain-clothes detectives, and assess the honesty of your employees, from management downward. Search the Internet using the key-word "mystery shopping service" for one in your area.

Customers Can Also Be Thieves - Common Scams

Not all fraud in the drinks industry is due to dishonest employees. Unfortunately, the environment of a beverage outlet makes it particularly vulnerable to customer theft. Understanding some of the possible ways in which dishonest guests can steal from your establishment helps you incorporate preventative procedures into your overall control system.

- **Taking advantage.** Customers will often take advantage of staff errors in calculating guest checks. A practical tip is to provide employees with calculators with printing tape for nonautomated transactions. A hard copy of the figures can provide useful evidence.

- **Transfer charges.** Dishonest guests may disclaim beverage charges incurred in other areas of the establishment. Make it a routine procedure for guests to sign all transfer checks upfront.

- **Property theft.** Guests often view stealing glassware or decorative furnishings from beverage outlets as a harmless prank. Turn this around. Offer embossed or customized items for sale at a modest price. Everybody wins. The establishment generates extra income and at the same time reduces the potential for theft-incurred costs.

- **Credit card fraud.** Make sure that all members of staff are fully informed of credit card processing procedures as stipulated by the credit card company.

- **Check fraud.** Managers should be trained to spot forged checks. All payments made by guests using personal or travelers checks should be monitored.

Beer can be lucrative for any beverage operation.

CHAPTER SEVEN

DRINK SELECTION

Develop a Successful Beer Program

Beer is a major seller in most bars, clubs and liquor outlets; it accounts for a hefty percentage of sales. Draft beer is particularly popular. It can prove a lucrative area of any beverage operation, if you get it right. It is estimated that wastage, spillage, excess foam, overpouring, poor quality, theft, giveaways and other draft-beer-related problems can drain your operation of an amazing 20 percent of inventory. Never underestimate the scope for cost reductions in this area!

- **Promotions.** Beer is a perishable product. As draft beer expires quickly, always consider discounting draft beer before bottled beer.

- **Computer-controlled draft beer technology.** A good control system is essential. The best type of control is a flow meter attached to each tap. If your usage is over two kegs per week, then you could justify the installation of an electronic device that counts fractions of an ounce. Take a look at the Berg Tap 1 Control system (www.berg-controls.com) and AzBar's product offerings (www.azbaramerica.com).

- **Foam head.** Control the size of the head and really make an impact on cost reductions. A good head of foam is essential, but it is up to you to control the depth of the foam. For example, in a 16-ounce glass, a half-inch head of foam yields around 136 glasses of draft per keg, whereas a one-inch head yields up to 152 glasses per keg. Add up the difference! Train all bartenders to achieve one-inch heads of foam.

- **Stop selling beer in pitchers.** Pitchers sell at a lower profit margin than beer by the glass. Although pitchers are a better deal for customers, they do little for your profitability. You're far better off selling four glasses of draft than one pitcher of beer.

Make the Right Choice of Wines

Choice of wine is a very individual matter. There are no rights and wrongs. It is important, however, to pander to customer preferences. Whether you run a bar, restaurant, club or specialized wine bar, you must purchase wine according to the demands of your clientele. If you get it right, profits will soar. But, if you choose wines that aren't a hit with your customers, you end up pouring your profits, as well as the unsold wine, down the drain.

- **Competition.** Look at the competition. Keep up to date with which wines are moving well. Read trade journals and publications, such as the "California Wine Growers Institute," to learn more about current trends, or consult the California Association of Wine Grape Growers: 555 University Avenue, Suite 250, Sacramento, CA 95825; www.cawg.org.

- **Review the wine list.** Be ruthless - if a wine is slow-moving, remove it from the list.

- **Get ahead of the crowd.** Introduce wines from up-and-coming wine regions. Suggestions include: New Zealand Riesling, Gewurztraminer and Sauvignon Blanc for whites, and South African Pinot Noir or Merlot for reds.

- **Storage.** Wine is a vulnerable product. One of the most effective ways of reducing costs and avoiding waste is to store wine in the correct environment (temperature, light and ventilation are particularly important). See www.storing-wine.com for handy tips on storing wine.

- **Opened bottles.** Establish par levels for each wine stocked behind the bar. Only open as many bottles as you need for one shift. All wines, particularly whites and cheaper house reds, become oxidized and deteriorate quickly once opened. A useful tip is not to pull the cork completely out of the bottle. If a cork is only partly pulled, the wine remains sealed, preventing oxygen from entering the bottle.

- **Cost controls on empty bottles.** Count empty wine bottles at the end of each shift. This practice makes sure that bartenders aren't overpouring. For example: you use six 1.5 liter bottles of wine during a shift; your standard portion for wine is 5 ounces; then sales for 60 to 61 glasses should show up on the register tape.

- **Discount premium wines.** Discounting premium wines results in a higher potential for profits. It also gives bartenders the opportunity to up-sell customers from standard house wines. This plan works well with "special buys" and wholesaler promotions.

Nonalcoholic Beverages - An Area of Opportunity

This sector of the beverage industry, known in the trade as NABs, needs to be taken very seriously if you want to cash in on current drinking trends. More customers today (often affluent, young, career-oriented clientele with plenty of disposable income) are choosing to drink NABs. Health issues, stricter DWI laws, and maybe even image are influencing their decisions to turn to NABs. The fact remains: this trend can mean big bucks. Tap into the possibilities:

- **Promotions.** Which NABs are consistently popular in your establishment? Buy bulk and sell on promotion. Publicize offers that your customers just cannot resist. Use a large chalkboard, or place "in-your-face" table tents on tables and at the bar.

- **Specialize.** Don't bother with expensive market research. Consult your regular customers. Ask them what they'd like to see on the menu. Decide on a few in-house specialties. Profits will increase noticeably, as margins for NABs are generally higher than for alcoholic beverages.

- **Bottled water.** This is no passing fad. Both in the dining room and at the bar, people are choosing to alternate alcoholic drinks with bottled water. Shelf dates tend to be generous (particularly for still, noncarbonated waters), so cash in: buy in bulk for big savings.

- **Added value.** Serve NABs in sophisticated, unusual glasses that scream "quality"! Customers will happily pay that little bit extra for a "wow" experience.

- **Don't price too low.** A word of warning. To make the most of this burgeoning area of the drinks market, keep your prices in line with your establishment's other alcoholic beverages. If NABs are priced too low, bartenders will be reluctant to promote them, and customers will think they're nothing special.

Cocktails - Reduce Costs While Increasing Customer Satisfaction

Cocktails are good for profits, and cocktail hour can be serious, big business. The customer feel-good factor is crucial. This can be achieved at no extra cost. Imagination is free.

- **Well brands.** Reduce costs by sticking to well brands for cocktails. Don't pour away your profits by using premium brands in cocktail recipes.

- **Premium brands.** Your establishment might be the sort of outlet that can make big profits out of selling premium brands. If so, use premium or middle-grade ingredients in your cocktails. Take every opportunity to advertise that fact. Emblazon quality brand names across your menus. Also, speak to your suppliers - they may be interested in offering you reduced rates in exchange for some free advertising.

- **Signature drinks.** Use your imagination and create something really special. Above all, a signature drink must look special. Choose unusual colors. Use different garnishes, such as asparagus, pepperoncini, jumbo shrimp, crab claw or scallions. Stand out from the crowd.

- **"Stirred, not shaken."** Don't shake mixed drinks that contain carbonated ingredients, particularly if those components are clear liquids. The bubbles will go flat, and the liquids will become cloudy. Stir instead.

- **Presentation.** Dare to be different. How about serving Chambord on the side for a Meltdown Raspberry Margarita? Let customers pour the liqueur portion themselves. As the liqueur blends into the drink, it will release wonderful aromatic raspberry flavors. It will also look visually stunning. Guests will think, "value."

- **Champagne.** Many recipes use champagne as a base ingredient. Once opened, a bottle of champagne or sparkling wine becomes a liability, because the bubbles are short-lived. Buy a bottle sealer specifically designed to cope with this problem. Ensure that bartenders know how to use it. You can't afford champagne wastage.

- **Ice.** Choose a cocktail station that has a deeper-than-average ice bin (up to 15 inches, maximum capacity). Put a divider through the middle of the bin and use it for storing both crushed and cubed ice. When the bar is busy, hanging around waiting for ice supplies costs money.

- **Speed.** Reposition liquor, wine and soda guns directly above the cocktail station. The soda gun should be placed on the left-hand side of the station, so that the bartender's right hand is free to hold a liquor bottle at the same time. A bartender using both hands is working at top speed and maximum efficiency.

- **Perceived value.** Improve customer perception of value and quality by increasing the high-cost portion of the cocktail. Up the liquor content to two ounces. Guests will feel they are getting real value for their money; you know this is good for profits.

Trim Liquor Costs

L iquor prices don't vary a great deal from one wholesaler to another. Packaging and size also tend to be fairly consistent. So, what can you do about reducing liquor costs in your operation? The answer is quite a lot! It's a misconception in the liquor trade that your options are limited when it comes to selling liquor. Consider the following opportunities:

- **Bulk buys.** Purchase staple liquors, such as whiskey, gin, vodka, brandy, rum and other popular spirits (e.g., fruit brandies) in bulk. They have a long shelf life and you know you can sell them within a reasonable period of time.

- **Trends.** Stay ahead of consumption trends. Respond quickly. For example, the current trend in the United States is toward "light" spirits such as 80-and 86-proof whiskies, instead of 100-proof (50 percent alcohol) bonded whiskies. Wholesalers, too, are keen to promote these alternatives.

- **Distilled spirits.** Their shelf life is exceptionally long. Buy distilled whenever possible, and minimize wastage.

- **Well liquors.** Which well liquors you choose can really make a difference in reducing costs. But don't buy at any price and compromise on quality.

Your reputation is at stake. Customers often judge an establishment by the quality of its well liquor.

- **Call liquors.** Increase margins on call liquors (brand names). Guests who ask for Gordon's gin or Jack Daniel's whiskey, for example, are loyal to the brand and will probably not question the price.

Choose Drink Mixes Carefully - Make an Impact on Cost Reductions

Just because mixes aren't a drink's main ingredients, one shouldn't ignore their impact upon your operation's profitability. There is considerable scope for trimming costs in this area. Despite being sold in small portions, drink mixes have a high overall sales volume; it is also predictable and consistent. Review the range of drink mixes used in your establishment. It all helps to reduce costs.

- **Fresh orange juice.** It is worth investing in a good commercial juicer for orange juice. A handy tip is to rinse oranges under hot water before placing them in the juicer - the juice yield will be higher.

- **From scratch drink mixes.** Preparing a whole range of drink mixes from scratch is too time-consuming, and all too often, results in inconsistent quality. You're better off buying ready-made mixes. Test samples of mixes before making a decision. Prepared mixes can vary considerably in taste and quality.

- **Cheat.** Have one drink mix that you prepare from scratch, say sweetened lemon juice. Promote its excellence. Customers will assume that because you make lemon juice from scratch, the same applies to all your other drink mixes.

- **Cut garnish costs.** Your choice of garnishes to accompany drink mixes can, quite literally, eat into your profits. Bartenders are notorious for nibbling olives, cherries, pineapple wedges, chocolate shavings, peppermint sticks, pretzels, etc. Remove temptation. Store garnishes in airtight containers in a cooler, away from temptation. Also, establish par levels for fruit garnishes and only prepare enough for one shift.

- **Unusual juices.** Use single-portion 6-ounce cans for less-frequently-served juices. Trade higher cost for reduced wastage, time saving and convenience.

Choosing the Right Suppliers for Your Beverage Requirements

A lot depends on your location. Some states have an almost monopolistic control over alcohol distribution; other states operate by licensing wholesalers. You need to familiarize yourself with county and local laws. They vary considerably from state to state. So, where do you start?

- **Source a supplier.** Take a look at your local beverage trade publications or Yellow Pages for a list of suppliers and wholesalers. The chances are you'll need to deal with several suppliers in order to get the full range of beverages required by your establishment.

- **Service.** As well as competitive prices, also look for exceptional service from your suppliers. For example, do they offer "emergency" deliveries at no extra cost to their regular customers? Time out to collect extra stock involves you in extra expense.

- **Visit warehouses.** Before deciding, visit a few different warehouses to see how they operate. More important, do they handle their stock with care? Bear in mind that returning faulty or poor merchandise can be time-consuming and expensive. Also, customer dissatisfaction is hard to quantify.

- **Beware of hidden charges for minimum orders.** Choose only a supplier that does not penalize you for minimum orders.

- **Pool buying.** If pool buying is legal in your state, choose a supplier that will give you the biggest savings. Negotiate, but don't compromise. Get a written quotation first.

Boost Profits By Choosing the Right Drink Recipes

The recipes you choose to feature on your drinks menu must do more than satisfy customer requirements. Plan carefully; a lot of thought needs to go also into keeping costs down, while at the same time maintaining a fine reputation for quality and imagination. This is no mean task, but the following simple suggestions may help:

- **Communicate your recipe preparation techniques.** Add a brief description about your unique preparation techniques underneath each recipe on the drinks menu. Tempt your customers to try "something different." The secret lies in your method of communication, rather than in the actual recipes themselves.

- **Highballs.** Although highballs can be served in a

variety of different-sized glasses, the ideal size for maximum efficiency and controlling costs is a 9-ounce glass. It accommodates the exact proportions for a standard highball recipe. The glass looks full to capacity; the customer is happy. Also, you know that the portions of ingredients are correct.

- **Recipes on napkins.** Dare to be different. Get some recipes you want to promote printed on napkins. It's different, and it's a good marketing tool. It also channels customers into ordering the recipes that you want them to buy. Choose the "special" recipes on the basis of higher profit margins, but promote them as "added value" recipes.

- **Mobile mini-bar.** As well as serving recipe drinks from the main bar, introduce a mini-bar on wheels. Get a bartender to wheel it around, selling "taster recipes" at promotional prices. The spontaneity of this approach is excellent for generating extra income.

Identify Loss-Leaders and Turn Them into Profit

You know exactly what stock you need to shift, but how do you do it? The way in which you choose to promote slow movers, stock where shelf dates are looming, or "mistake" purchases can mean the difference between profit and loss. Treat promotions as more than a damage-limitation exercise: you can actually make money out of loss leaders.

- **Image.** Promote your chosen drink (or recipe) as something "hot," "clever" and "smart." Simple flattery never fails; it is one the best promotional tools available. Word your advert to imply that this drink is "ahead of the crowd"!

- **Oversized glassware.** You want to shift volume - and you want to shift it fast. So, serve promotions in specialty, oversized glassware. Play on the fun element of presentation. For example, if you're trying to promote a certain beer, serve it in chunky 16-ounce beer mugs. Invent a novel name for the glass, such as "Hefty Handful"!

- **Glowing neon serving trays** - a real talking point, and younger clientele love them. For maximum effect, keep the bar lighting low. The emphasis will be on presentation rather than the loss-leader drinks you're trying to shift. Contact Glo-Tray at 203-226-3090 for further information.

- **Timing and exclusivity.** Timing is the key to exclusivity. Only offer specials at a certain time of day and on certain days. A good move is to avoid "Happy Hour" altogether. Customers think of this period as cheap and cheerful, but nothing special. Instead, choose to promote your loss leaders at a time when the bar is buzzing, perhaps on a Friday or Saturday evening.

Choose Well Liquors Wisely - Mistakes Can Bankrupt Your Business

Well liquors are probably the most important products in any successful beverage operation. Approximately 50 percent of a typical bar's liquor depletion comes from well liquor. Therefore, how you select, handle and sell these liquors is crucial to the long-term sustainability of your operation. Bear in mind the following:

- **Avoid supplier "come-ons."** Suppliers are always keen to off-load excess stocks of well liquor. Only succumb if you think that you can easily sell the extra volume at a significant profit.

- **Quality.** Consistency and quality of well liquors varies considerably. Two factors are really important when choosing which well liquors to sell: quality and cost. Select well liquors that exactly match the quality expectations of your clientele. If your customers are picky, you cannot skimp on quality. It would cost you too dearly.

- **Sequence.** The traditional liquor sequence (bourbon, whiskey, gin, vodka, rum, tequila), where dark liquors are separated from light liquors, isn't the most cost-effective method of sequencing your well liquor. Try the more modern approach. Alternate light and dark liquors, e.g., gin, bourbon, vodka, scotch, etc. It reduces costly wastage. Bartenders are less likely to mistake one well liquor for another.

- **Well liquor grade.** Match the grade of well liquor to your type of establishment. No need for costly overkill. For example, exclusive clubs may have no choice but to sell predominantly premium brands. Less image-conscious outlets can reduce costs by selling semi-premium or pouring brands.

Employees need to be many things, including polite, personable and hardworking.

CHAPTER EIGHT

STAFF RECRUITMENT, MANAGEMENT & TRAINING

Good Staff Is a Business's Greatest Asset - Hire the Best

Any beverage outlet is highly dependent upon the quality of its staff. Employees need to be multi-talented: honest, hardworking, reliable, prepared to work unsociable hours, friendly, polite and oozing hospitality - a tall order! Be realistic. Rapid expansion within the hospitality sector in recent years has created a flood of new bartender jobs. This means that job seekers are picky about where they work; but so must you, the recruiter, be picky about whom you employ. Avoid the following pitfalls.

- **Employee rights.** Strict federal and state regulations govern employment procedures. Get an attorney to check out your terms of contract and hiring procedures. A vindictive employee (or ex-employee) could cost you dearly.

- **Recruitment advertisement.** There are laws that govern what can and cannot be stated in a recruitment advertisement. Above all, avoid violating discrimination laws regarding sex, age, nationality and minority groups.

- **Staff selection.** Cut out the cost of advertising in newspapers, etc. One of the best ways to attract new staff is to ask existing bartenders you trust if they know of anyone looking for a job. Their suggestions are likely to be productive.

- **Incentives.** Offer reliable staff an incentive for "recruiting" the right person - say, for example, if they recruit someone who successfully manages to complete his or her first three months on the job.

- **Shop the competition.** Check out the opposition. Watch their bartenders in action. If you like what you see, don't be afraid to offer an incentive to come and work for you. It's human nature to do a good job if you've been "head-hunted."

- **Ongoing recruitment.** Staff turnover in the beverage industry is notoriously high. Save time and money by maintaining an open job application file. Remain alert to recruitment possibilities. Oftentimes, potential employees who approach you are already familiar with your establishment and its clientele. More than likely, they will fit in well.

Tips for Reducing Labor Costs

The key to controlling labor costs is to retain a stable, reliable and happy workforce. In today's beverage industry, it's becoming increasingly difficult to recruit and retain a cadre of good staff. The cost involved in replacing employees is considerable. This creates a vicious circle. Management needs to allocate sufficient funds for creating desirable working conditions. It must also offer attractive pay packages while, at the same time, strive to reduce overall operational costs. Focus on the following crucial issues:

- **Help new employees get to grips with the job.** Whatever it takes (advice, training, supervision), make sure that new members of staff are operating to maximum capacity as quickly as possible. So much money is wasted if new recruits don't know what they're supposed to be doing.

- **Offer a benefits package that is better than the competition.** Regard this as a long-term investment. It will reduce staff turnover, thus reducing overall costs. "Extras" don't have to be costly. Consider, for example, additional in-house training or extra vacation time.

- **Treat all staff as human beings.** Recognize and praise their efforts whenever you can. It costs you nothing. What it does is help you to avoid the expense of recruiting and retraining new members of staff.

- **Tips.** Reward exceptional performance with a larger share of the tips. Extra cash in hand is one of the best motivators. A happy employee will remain loyal to your establishment.

How You Train New Employees Can Have a Major Impact upon Your Business

No area of management offers greater scope for increased employee productivity and healthy profits than effective training. Forget the assumption that training is expensive. It need not be. Sending your staff away on formal training courses can indeed prove costly. But, the best form of training - the training that will really make a difference - can be carried out in-house, at no extra cost. Good first impressions on new employees can really make a difference:

- **Start training immediately.** When a new employee walks through the door, don't keep him or her hanging around. However busy you are, nothing can be more important than making the new recruit feel welcome and enthusiastic about "joining the team."

- **Allocate the function of training to an experienced and trusted member of staff.** This works! The trainer feels honored and the trainee feels he or she has someone to turn to with queries, without "bothering" management all the time.

- **Timing.** Choose quiet times to go through the specific routines and requirements of the job. Also, make sure that you have the time to give each new employee an overview of the operation. Productivity improves if employees feel they are more than a cog in a wheel.

- **Orientation program.** All employees should be given a specific job description, plus information about all the issues that affect their performance. Examples of the latter include information on periodic or annual performance reviews, emergency procedures, disciplinary and grievance procedures, personal conduct issues, work schedule expectations and availability of additional training.

Front-of-House Management Tips

Hands-on front-of-house management is central to the success of your enterprise. Never underestimate the impact that a skilled floor manager can have on the profitability of your establishment. Sweeping changes aren't necessary; what does make a difference is attention to detail. Have you thought of the following?

- **Smile.** Greet regular customers by name and ask them meaningful questions that make them feel treated as individuals. If one of your regulars is in the hospital, send "Get Well" greetings from the establishment.

- **Entrance.** Make sure the entrance to your establishment is clean and welcoming. Position an interesting feature, such as a sculpture or painting, near the door. It makes a good talking point and sets you apart from the competition.

- **Role model.** How you react to customers will set a standard for your employees. Lead by example. Customers' impressions of your bar are directly affected by the service they receive from your employees.

- **New customers.** Try to meet new customers each shift. Add their names to your customer mailing list. Exchange business cards.

- **Exceed expectations.** Be prepared to help out when it's busy. Take cocktail orders or even help behind the bar with bottle opening, barrel changing or glass washing.

- **Impress customers.** Ask customers how they'd like their drinks mixed and served. Some have strong preferences for a particular type of glassware. Others are fussy about the balance of dry and sweet ingredients. Demonstrate concern for individual tastes - it's guaranteed to impress!

- **Pre-shift meeting.** A few minutes spent with the bar staff setting goals for the shift is time well spent. Enlist the support of your team. Keep them briefed. Always welcome two-way communication.

- **Lasting impressions.** As customers leave, open the door for them. Thank them for coming. Leave them with a favorable impression that makes them want to return.

Ongoing Training Is One of the Most Effective Ways of Retaining Staff

It is common courtesy to offer your employees ongoing training. It is also crucial to the profitability of your operation. You want to keep good staff and avoid the unnecessary expense of constant recruitment and re-training. Managers who demonstrate a positive attitude about ongoing training are more likely to retain a loyal team of motivated employees.

- **Plan.** Take the time and trouble to plan training sessions. Make sure that they are relevant - not just paying lip service to the general notion of training. Time spent planning training sessions is time well spent.

- **Set times for training.** Allocate a set time for on-going training sessions. Most employees want to do a good job and will look forward to taking part in these fixed, mutually beneficial sessions.

- **Keep it simple.** Ongoing training programs don't have to be complicated. In fact, the simpler, the better. A basic training session could include the following:
  1. Trainer chooses either: a) an area of the operation that needs attention, e.g., "How to avoid lines of customers building up at the bar"

or b) invites an open discussion about how routine daily procedures could be improved.

2. Trainer must be observed listening to suggestions and acting upon them.

3. Trainers also should use the session as an opportunity to identify individual employee training requirements. A relaxed atmosphere that invites open dialog is essential.

4. After the session, the trainer must address points raised, plus any individual employee training needs. This must be accomplished in as informal and positive manner as possible.

Winning Personal Serving Techniques - Set High Standards

Don't assume that all employees are natural communicators who can instinctively generate an ambiance of generous hospitality. Some can; the majority, however, require clear guidelines. Indeed, most employees prefer to know exactly what's expected of them. As well as insisting that servers greet customers with a pleasant smile, you can suggest several other techniques that can make a big difference. Try the following:

- **Individual greetings.** Servers need to introduce themselves by name, at some point during the greeting. But, to make a really good impression, insist that their first words are NOT the standard: "Hi, my name is. How can I help you?" This type of greeting is far too commonplace. Ask staff to think first, then adopt a more individual approach. Suggest they slip their name into the conversation, towards the end of the greeting. It works!

- **Personal interest.** If a bartender recognizes a "regular," he or she should always address that person by name and engage him or her in conversation about things that are of real interest to that guest.

- **Let serving staff take the initiative.** Give your serving staff a free hand to enhance customer service. After all, they're in a strong position to identify potential problems or areas in which service can be improved. Support their decisions, as far as you can.

- **Keep personal problems under wraps.** An unhappy employee may be tempted to bemoan their lot to a willing listener. Sorry, but servers should be instructed to hide their problems behind a smile until their shift is over.

- **Comfort factor.** Fine hospitality involves more than leaning on the bar chatting with customers. Guest comfort matters. Small actions, such as removing dirty glasses, cleaning ashtrays and wiping tables at regular intervals, can significantly enhance customer satisfaction. It encourages guests to linger and spend more money in your establishment.

- **Balance.** Servers need to be told how to strike a balance between attentiveness and neglect. They should be taught when to approach customers to see whether they're ready for the next round of drinks.

- **Limit damage when ejecting a drunken or abusive patron.** Avoid making a scene. Try to calm the aggressor by making a positive gesture. Volunteer to phone for a cab. Pour the customer a free cup of coffee or a soft drink - in a quieter area of the establishment. Keep the patron's pride intact.

Practical Tips for Training Bartenders

In practice, training bartenders often can be a haphazard affair: too much advice, too little, or worse - all theory and nothing that is of any practical use to them once they're standing behind the bar, with a line of impatient customers waiting to be served. Before you let a new employee loose on your precious customers, make sure that he or she really understands and is competent in the following five main areas:

- **Cash procedures.** Ensure that all bartenders fully understand and stick to establishment procedures for all money transactions. They must be completely competent at operating the cash register. There is no room for ambiguity of training in this area.

- **Dispense liquor efficiently.** Train bartenders to use equipment, and familiarize them with how each drink should be prepared.

- **Bar inventory.** Show them how to record stock, enter details on the perpetual inventory, requisition replacement stock and deal with empties and where to locate each beverage behind the bar.

- **Speed.** Make it quite clear that, under normal circumstances, bartenders are expected to pour drinks quickly and in a fixed amount of time. Define times that are appropriate to your establishment.

- **Cleanliness.** Spell it out. Bartenders must abide by house standards.

Employee Mismanagement Can Bankrupt Your Business

Poor management results in low staff morale, absenteeism and an increased incidence of internal theft. And that's just for starters! It can also put you out of business, fast. Learn to anticipate potential management problems. Tackle minor issues before they get out of control. Watch out especially for the following warning signals:

- **Favoritism.** Does the manager appear to be acting unfairly or irrationally towards certain members of staff? Maybe the manager is letting other employees get away with poor time keeping or offering them free drinks, for instance. Inconsistent behavior on the part of management is guaranteed to affect productivity adversely.

- **Public verbal reprimands.** Never tolerate verbal reprimands by management in front of customers or fellow employees. Disciplinary issues should be dealt with in private, at the end of the shift.

- **Lack of guidance.** The business will suffer at the hands of incompetent staff. General morale will also plummet. "Hands-on" guidance and constructive supervision are essential ingredients of any successful management strategy.

- **Lack of respect.** Managers who show a lack of respect for fellow employees create a negative atmosphere that is detrimental to the smooth running of the establishment. Managers should also categorically avoid making sexual advances towards certain members of personnel or making derogatory or embarrassing comments about any member of staff.

- **Lack of support.** It is the duty of a manager to acknowledge and praise good performance. He or she is also obliged to resolve any work-related disagreements. Turning a blind eye just won't do.

Bartender Recruitment and Selection Tips

The cost of hiring the wrong bartender can actually cripple your business. Unfortunately, however, even if you put a great deal of thought and preparation into your recruitment plan, it can still go horribly wrong. In practice, selection is really a process of elimination. Rarely is it a case of "Yes - I just know I've chosen the right person!" View recruitment as something of a damage-limitation exercise. You won't go far wrong.

- **Avoid hasty decisions.** Don't rush into replacing a bartender if an existing member of staff leaves suddenly. Recruit in haste; repent at leisure!

- **Avoid using generic job application forms.** Think about what makes your establishment "tick." What types of employees are best at realizing its success? Define candidate requirements accordingly.

- **Test applicants' specific knowledge of the beverage industry.** For example, can they identify a wide range of spirits? How much do they know about the origins and main characteristics of different wines? Do they know what the minimum drinking age is and what constitutes acceptable forms of identification?

- **Practical test.** Talking to candidates will only get you so far. Take them into the bar and ask them to perform a simple dexterity test, such as pouring a glass of draft beer. Don't expect miracles, but it will give you some indication of their suitability.

- **Consult existing members of staff.** Try to engineer a situation where, at some point during the interview, fellow bartenders can take a sneak preview. It is vitally important that the interviewee "fits in" with the rest of the team.

- **Attitude.** Ask questions that are likely to expose a candidate's true work ethic. How many hours a week do they need to work (as opposed to want to work)? Also, how much money do they actually need to earn? These types of questions are excellent indicators of future commitment.

Keep Staff Happy - Keep Labor Costs Down

It costs nothing to treat employees with respect and consideration. Treat them as professionals, and they will reward you with loyalty and a sense of commitment. This means, of course, that you won't have to worry so much about the time-consuming and alarmingly expensive business of recruiting and training new staff. Remind yourself, daily, of the following opportunities to maintain a positive and amicable working environment:

- **Don't raise false hopes.** When you offer someone work as a bartender, don't oversell the job or idealize the establishment. This will result only in disillusionment when reality sets in.

- **Consistent behavior.** Working in the beverage industry can often prove stressful for management and bar staff alike. Management, however, must be seen to behave consistently. In particular, make sure that all employees abide by the establishment's policies and set procedures. No one should be allowed to "cut corners." Favoritism leads to overwhelming resentment.

- **Avoid social involvement.** Associating with fellow employees outside working hours ruins your credibility as a manager.

- **Money talks.** The easier you make it for employees to earn more money, the happier they will be and the less likely to move on to another job. Distribute tips as generously as possible. Pay over the odds for extra time worked. It will save you money long-term and also reduce the temptation for internal theft.

Review the working environment to find ways to cut costs.

CHAPTER NINE

OTHER OPPORTUNITIES TO CONTROL COSTS IN THE BEVERAGE INDUSTRY

The Working Environment - Cunning Cost-Reducing Tips

Take a fresh look at all aspects of your working environment. It's so easy to overlook the obvious when you're preoccupied with the day-to-day details of running a busy beverage operation. There is always room for improvement, in every establishment. The opportunity for reducing costs, will surprise you.

- **Reduce the likelihood of workers' compensation claims.** Introduce preventive measures, such as rubber mats behind the bar to avoid slipping, safety gadgets for bartenders who have to slice fruit and garnishes, back supports for staff who have to move heavy kegs of beer, etc.

- **Control heating and air-conditioning.** Put timers and locks on all thermostats. Make sure that staff cannot override the settings.

- **Safeguard the CO_2 gas system.** Avoid costly accidents (and excess spillage). Equip your gas pressure regulator with a pressure-relief device that is fitted with a release valve. Excess pressure builds up quickly if the equipment is not properly controlled. This can lead to barrels exploding and serious accidents.

- **Alarm buttons.** Anticipate fights breaking out. Install concealed alarm triggers behind the bar. Have backup management on hand to intervene and recover the situation before any damage is done.

- **Security guard.** Employ a security guard. This is not a major expense. Indeed, a reliable guard is a sound investment. By monitoring people wandering in and out of your establishment, as well as spotting insider theft at all levels, he or she can make a major contribution to keeping costs down.

Extra Cost-Reducing Serving Tips

The service need not suffer. Customer satisfaction remains high. A few well-disguised shortcuts will reduce costs and may, at the same time, improve overall efficiency. Consider the following small changes to your drink serving routines.

- **Acrylic glassware.** Suitability depends on the type of establishment, but you'd be surprised at the number of establishments where acrylic glassware is perfectly acceptable. In fact, it is often preferable at outdoor outlets such as sports venues. It doesn't break; it's cheaper; and bartenders can "scoop ice" easily using acrylic glasses. (One action saves time, big time!) Also, customers are not as tempted to steal "disposable" glasses.

- **Premix Bloody Marys.** It's too time consuming to make your own. Consistency can be an issue if different bartenders don't stick to the recipe. Buy Bloody Marys premixed. The quality is every bit as good.

- **Garnishes.** In a time warp? Go for cheaper fruit that's in season. Or, review bulk-buying less-expensive yet more eye-catching decorative flags, etc.

- **Frozen drinks.** Reduce the amount of liquor in frozen drinks. The law doesn't specify that the liquor content be 1 ounce or 1-1/4 ounces. The choice is yours.

- **Mixers.** Use off-brand mixers, such as lime juice and grenadine.

- **Draft beers.** Spillage is extremely high for draft beers. Introduce ounce-counting technology; make it a priority.

Extra Cost-Reducing Staffing Tips

It may, at first, seem hard to save on staffing costs, but in the interests of long-term survival, you have no choice. Only the owner or manager sees the overall picture and can make these decisions. After all, your employees want to be in a job this time next year!

- **Unpaid breaks.** Employment law requires that employers must give their employees a 30-minute break after a continuous four-hour shift. But what is not so commonly known is that employers are not obliged to pay for this break.

- **Smoking.** Smoking breaks definitely should be unpaid. They add up over the course of a shift. What's more, non-smoking employees harbor resentment for this break privilege, particularly if it's paid.

- **Daily labor costs.** Review labor costs daily and for each shift. Send employees home early if business is quiet.

- **Staff leasing.** Consider the benefits of leasing your employees to a staff leasing company. It offers you flexibility and significant savings on your annual workers' compensation premium and unemployment compensation rate. Staff leasing companies will also do your payroll and carry out most human resources functions for you. Employees also benefit with realistic medical insurance, for instance. Everyone wins. For further information about staff leasing, call 800-447-4383.

Dispensing Draft Beer - Extra Cost-Reducing Tips

No beverage offers greater potential for wastage and spillage than draft beer. The opportunities to cut costs in this area are, therefore, considerable. Consider the following facts: Draft beer pours at 2 ounces per second. Cost varies between approximately 2.5 cents and 8 cents per ounce, depending upon brand and beverage outlet. Therefore, using a 10-ounce glass, a spillage or overpour of 10 percent will occur in just half a second or less. Multiply this, in terms of lost income. Worrying? These suggestions will help you recover the situation:

- **Practical evaluation.** First, get some facts. Measure how much draft beer is served in your glasses and pitchers. Count how many kegs you purchase weekly. Calculate how much beer you actually sell during the same period. The difference will surprise you.

- **Install a flow meter.** It measures the exact amount of beer served in each glass, mug or pitcher. It also records the amount of beer poured at each draft tap during each shift. Visit www.auper.com/DispensingDraft or www.berg-controls.com.

- **Use the flow meter report at the end of each shift.** Identify problems immediately. Reduce your pour costs and maximize your profits simultaneously.

- **Install an empty beer keg detector.** These detectors will automatically shut down the line when a keg is empty, keeping beer in the line while a new keg is hooked up, thus preventing excess loss of draft beer.

Extra Tips for Establishing a Successful Wine Program

In recent years there's been an explosion in the sale of wines worldwide, but particularly in the United States. Wine bars, too, are becoming increasingly popular nowadays, especially with the young and affluent. A recent survey concluded that in bars and restaurants, white wine was the number-one choice of American women. It was also the third-most-popular drink (after beer and margaritas) ordered by American men. In other words, there are big bucks to be made from selling wine. The following suggestions should give you a head start.

- **House wine.** The most important wine on the wine list. It's the standard by which the rest of the wines on your list will be judged. If you don't know much about wine, seek expert advice. A wrong decision could ruin your reputation. It could also make a serious dent in your wine sales and profits.

- **Gross profits.** As wine tends to sell at a higher cost percentage than beer, it yields more dollars in profits. Without taking advantage, you should be able to up the margins even further without customers noticing. Wine drinkers are often more concerned with taste and image.

- **Glass size.** Encourage wine sales by serving wine in the correct-shaped glasses. Wine drinkers tend to know their stuff! For example, red wine should always be served in a bowl-shaped glass with sufficient space between the rim and the level of the wine for the "connoisseur" to swirl the content and sample the bouquet.

- **Standard portions.** Adopt a standard-sized pour of 6 ounces for a glass of wine. Serve the portion in an 8-ounce glass. The glass will be three-quarters full. The bartender is more likely to pour the exact amount, and the customer is likely to be happy with the presentation.

Shop the Opposition

Call it market research. Shopping the opposition is one of the cheapest and best ways of working out a marketing strategy for your operation. However, successful "shopping" involves more than copying your competitors' ideas. You need to be realistic. Take an objective look at your own operation. Ask yourself where exactly you should position yourself in relation to your direct competition. How do customers perceive your respective businesses? Identify your market position.

- **Enter a competitor's establishment and sit at the bar.** Listen to the regulars, particularly those "bar hoppers," who like to think they're an authority on every bar in the neighborhood. They'll give you all the information you need - and more!

- **Shop on a regular basis.** After all, you do want a representative sample, and you need to keep up to date. Remember, the beverage industry can be very fickle; bars go in and out of favor all the time.

- **Don't be sneaky.** When you get a chance, introduce yourself as the manager from down the road. Compliment their establishment. Be positive. The "Mr. Nice Guy" approach works better long-term. You also may attract some new customers to your establishment - or even find their good bartenders knocking on your door for a job!

Key information: when shopping the competition, look out for the following:

- **Stock.** What quality liquor do they carry in the well: pouring, call or premium? Do they carry anything you don't? What beer labels do they offer? What is their house wine?

- **Pricing.** From highballs to beer to wine - you need to know.

- **Marketing.** What sorts of promotions are they running? Do they sell a popular product that you don't?

- **Ambiance.** Note the background music, the seating arrangements and the lighting. Do they offer entertainment? If so, what type?

- **Staff.** Do they appear better trained and motivated?

- **Glassware and portions.** How do they dispense alcohol: automatic or free-pour? How big are their wine portions? Do they use beer pitchers? If so, what size?

Banquet Beverages - Tips for Reducing Costs but Not Quality

The main type of alcoholic beverage sold at banquets is bottled wine - and there's a lot you can do to maximize profits in this area, without lowering standards. The usual format involves a fixed number of bottles placed on each table. The host/customer then pays for the total number of bottles opened by the end of the banquet. Here are a few suggestions for reducing costs:

- **Improve stock control.** Stick to a "fixed number of bottles" agreement. Some hosts prefer to offer payment per glass, but this method is best avoided, if possible. The "total bottles" approach gives both you and the customer better control of the situation.

- **Reduce staffing costs.** Encourage the guests to pour their own wine at the table. It appears more generous toward the guests. It also saves on staffing costs.

- **Champagne toasts.** If a champagne toast is called for, and the host has no strong views on the matter, serve a quality sparkling wine instead. Despite being a cheaper product, the scope for heftier markups is there for the taking. Also, the perceived quality of a top-of-the-range sparkling wine is far superior to mediocre champagne. Some of the best sparkling whites today are being produced by subsidiaries of champagne producers.

- **Cash bar.** Most banquets operate a cash bar, where patrons can purchase additional drinks. Bartenders have to handle a lot of cash in an "open" environment. The opportunity for theft and alcohol abuse is rife. Put only your most trustworthy staff in charge of a banquet cash bar.

Market Your New Bar - Profit-Boosting Tips

Don't feel you've got to throw big bucks into marketing your new bar. It can be achieved on a shoestring. Careful planning and a dash of inspiration are all that's required. Also, after the initial promotion it's important to keep up the good work. Seize every opportunity to market your establishment. View marketing as an essential part of your ongoing business strategy.

- **Image.** Concentrate on projecting a distinct image for your bar. Choose a simple eye-catching logo. Perhaps design the logo yourself. Use a home computer to print out your menus and table tent promotions, with the logo emblazoned at the head.

- **Promote yourself as proprietor.** Make people want to drink at your bar. Involve yourself in your neighborhood community. Support local charities. Join the local chamber of commerce.

- **Pre-opening publicity.** Organize a pre-opening get-together. Invite all those people you think can add to the long-term success of your operation: suppliers, competitors, local business persons, civic leaders, etc. It is so important that they are the first to enjoy what your establishment has to offer.

- **Teaser campaign.** About six weeks before you open, introduce billboards, banners or bumper stickers with a hint at something exciting about to happen. For example, "JUMPIN' JACKS IS COMING...SOON!!"

- **Press release.** Write your own press release. Or get someone clever with words to write it for you. Send it to the local newspaper. Phone the newspaper's publicity department as the official opening date approaches and remind them that you're about to open this exciting new venture. It's worth being pushy just to get all this free publicity.

- **Professional Web site.** An attractive Web site is an excellent promotional tool. Consult the professionals. Try The House of Blues: www.houseofblues.com, or Hooters: www.hooters.com. Both can point you in the right direction. Also, how about using your Web site to boost sales by merchandising your in-house products? Use your Web site to give directions, build a mailing list and post employee schedules.

- **Signage.** Get noticed. Neon signage is guaranteed to do the job. Contact your suppliers: they may be prepared to help out in exchange for you promoting their products.

Extra Tips for Streamlining Your Bar Par Procedures

An accurate and well-maintained bar par is at the heart of any successful beverage operation. Discrepancies or sloppy management in this area - and your business is doomed. Consider the following suggestions:

- **"Sheet-to-shelf."** Arrange bottles behind the bar in the same order as they appear on the liquor requisition form and the monthly inventory form. This approach is both time- and cost-effective.

- **Triplicate bar par record sheets.** Record bar par totals on a triplicate record set. Keep one copy behind the bar, one in the beverage storeroom and one in the manager's storeroom. This is not overkill. It makes it much easier to resolve disputes and discrepancies at a later date.

- **One shift at a time.** Ideally, keep sufficient full bottles behind the bar to last you for one shift. If, in practice, this isn't feasible, make sure that NO MORE than one day's worth of stock is stored behind the bar.

- **Weekly pouring cost inventory.** Check your pouring costs (PCs) weekly. It helps reduce costs by maintaining tight bar par controls. Simply total the cost value of your requisitions for the week and then divide this figure by total liquor sales for the week. The difference should be no greater than 1.5 percent of normal monthly PCs.

- **Counting empty bottles.** Ask bartenders to place all their empties on top of the bar at the end of each shift. It's the quickest and easiest way to see if bar and requisition totals tally.

Encourage Bartenders to Do More than Serve - Encourage Them to Sell, As Well!

You've trained your bar staff; they know what drinks to serve and how to serve them. They even know quite a lot about the product. So, why not put this knowledge to good use? Encourage your bartenders to do more than answer customer queries about products and serve them. Train employees to adopt a "suggest sale" approach. It will boost profits instantly.

- **Offer incentives.** Reward staff that actively sell your products with whatever you know they would appreciate - perhaps better shifts or a small raise.

- **New products.** Suggest that bartenders promote new products with lead-in questions, such as: "Would you be interested in trying our special house wine/recipe/draft beer?"

- **Get bar staff to up-sell liquor.** If a customer orders a highball, try to channel him or her in the direction of a premium brand label. For example, if the customer requests a gin and tonic, the bartender could reply, "Would that be Gordon's, Sir/Madam?"

- **Product knowledge.** Encourage bartenders to use their product knowledge. Customers enjoy discussing the merits of the drink that they have just ordered. A little reinforcement that they've made a wise decision goes a long way towards generating repeat sales.

Surprise Your Customers with New Ideas on a Regular Basis

The element of surprise can work wonders. Customers like to know that you're always keen to welcome them through your doors. But, above all, they appreciate your attention to detail and the fact that you want to please. Novelty is always good for profitability. Subtlety, however, is the key. Keep "surprises" simple and don't let them intrude upon the general ambiance of your establishment.

- **Inspiration.** Always be on the lookout for new ideas that will keep you on top of current trends and promotions. Attend trade shows where they have useful seminars on a wide range of topics related to the beverage industry. For example, the National Licensed Beverage Association holds annual conventions in about twenty states; for further information, contact the NLBA at 800-441-9894.

- **VIP cards.** Convert one-off customers to regulars. VIP membership cards aren't expensive to produce in bulk. Invest in the magnetic strip version. Apart from bringing in extra revenue, they can provide you with the information to set up a mailing system - a real win-win situation.

- **Jukebox.** Tried and tested, the jukebox appeals to a wide range of clientele. It also brings in the crowds. A word of warning though - avoid the "package" type of jukebox, where the machine comes prestacked with music supplied by a vendor. Make your own selection. Fill it with discs that you know your customers will enjoy.

- **Darts.** If you have the space, consider introducing a new-technology version of the old favorite pub game: the dartboard. Coin-operated dart systems are becoming increasingly popular nowadays. Introduce a darts tournament on a slack night.

- **Pool table.** Install a pool table in a back-room bar. As with darts, pool never goes out of fashion. Better still, it is likely to draw a faithful crowd who will become regular drinkers at your establishment. After the initial investment, pool tables are easy to maintain and don't need regular updating.

- **Coin-operated entertainment.** Introduce a couple of profit-based coin-operated machines. It costs you nothing. All suppliers require is a share of the profit. Not bad, considering you don't have to shell out on installation or maintenance costs.

- **Floater liquors and glass giveaways.** Introduce specialty drinks with novelty give-away glasses (if you can strike a good deal). For example, have a frozen drink promotion, where you add a half shot as a float of liquor on top of the drink, for a small extra charge of, say, $1.50.

- **Bar snack "nibblers."** Create a few simple and inexpensive snack dishes to complement whatever drinks are on promotion. Arrange them in small bowls on the bar, e.g., German "wurst" with Beck's Dark beer, or olives with a simple Italian "Vino Da Tavola." Tip: keep the bowls small - customers won't want to appear greedy in company!

- **Vending machines with a difference.** Focus on your customer requirements. Is there any extra product they would appreciate apart from the usual vending machine offerings? Consider

additional lines of toiletries, antacids, aspirins,
breath mints - whatever you think would appeal.
Try harder to please your regular patrons.

- **Staff uniforms.** Alternate the color of their shirts
  on a regular basis. Customers will notice. Or, use
  brewery's give-away promotional T-shirts to
  promote whatever drinks you're trying to off-load!

- **New items.** Have a "new item" section on the
  menu that changes every week, without fail. Build
  up such an impressive repertoire of "new" ideas
  that eventually you'll be able to "recycle" the "new"
  ideas without anyone noticing!

Streamline Bar Layout

A well-designed and compact bar will directly affect
bartender productivity. If the layout of the
workstation is carefully planned, bartenders will be able
to function to maximum capacity, saving time and
money that could be better deployed in other areas of
your establishment. Here are a few suggestions to make
the bartender's life a lot easier:

- **Position of ingredients.** Every ingredient required
  to fulfill a drinks order should be located within a
  6-foot radius of the bartender's position in front of
  the workstation. This 6-foot radius represents a
  step and an arm's reach.

- **Effective use of space.** Equipment should be
  positioned so that the bartender is able to
  complete the drinks order with the least number of
  actions. Wasted movements mean wasted time and
  profits.

- **Well liquor.** Place well liquors in a "speed rack" mounted to the front of the workstation. Easy access is essential.

- **Premium liquors and liqueurs.** Position these high-margin drinks where they are clearly visible and enticing to customers, but, at the same time, away from the immediate serving area of the busy bartender. A good location is on the back bar at approximately 42 inches above bar level.

- **Shelving.** Display-case shelves should be wide enough to accommodate bottles two-deep. Design shelves that are between 12- and 16-inches deep. This will make the most of the available storage space behind the bar.

- **Minimize "cross-handed" actions.** As most employees are right-handed, position glasses to the left of the bar. Right-handed bartenders will instinctively reach for the bottle with their right hand and the glass with their left.

- **Glassware.** Glassware should be stored to the left of the workstation, with the most frequently used glasses within easy bartender reach.

- **Lighting.** Adequate lighting is essential for accurate drink making. A good idea is to fix fluorescent strip lighting just beneath the bar top.

Sales Are Slumping, Trade Is Dwindling - So, What Do You Do Next?

You can't quite put your finger on it. You've investigated all the obvious possibilities - bar pars, perpetual inventory, stockroom, security, labor costs, purchasing levels, stock rotation, wastage, thieving, etc., but you're still none the wiser? Oftentimes, the answer lies in that almost-intangible element of "quality, superior service." Take a another look at the following aspects of your operation and ask yourself the following questions. Be honest. Small changes can make a big difference.

- **Product knowledge.** Hand on heart - do you genuinely know everything about every product that you sell in your establishment? If the manager doesn't, what hope can you have for front-of-house servers!

- **Attention and recognition.** Are your bartenders in a rut? Do they serve customers with the appearance of being on "auto pilot"? Do they attach greater importance to making the drink than tending to the customer? Easily done in a busy bar, but customers who are treated like numbers will take their trade elsewhere.

- **Up-selling.** Are all your bartenders fully trained to up-sell ROUTINELY, not just for promotional drinks? "Suggestive selling" should be second nature to all servers and management alike - at all times.

- **Make the most of new customers.** Do bartenders spend too much time talking either to each other or to a handful of regulars and simply ignore the "untapped" potential of new guests?

- **Environment.** Are your employees exhibiting sloppy habits in front of customers? For example, do they eat, smoke or chat noisily amongst themselves, in front of guests?

- **Encourage patrons to linger longer.** Turn negative into positive. A simple move that works well is to make sure that staff ask customers the right questions. For example, instead of "Would you like the bill?", direct employees to ask, "May I get you another round of (whatever the customers happen to be drinking)?"

- **Headset communication.** In a busy bar or club, consider issuing serving staff radio headsets. They can be great time savers for both staff and customers. Also, the equipment will not seem obtrusive in a large, noisy environment.

- **Negative image.** Basic question: Are the rest rooms clean? If they are unhygienic, customers can boycott your establishment for that reason alone. Also, are intoxicated customers or potential fights anticipated and dealt with as quickly as possible? No one feels comfortable drinking in an unpleasant environment.

- **Provide Internet access.** Install an Internet terminal in a quiet area of your bar. Keep it separate from the main floor but close enough to the bar so that customers will be tempted to combine business with pleasure! If your establishment already has the infrastructure for Internet access, the cost of an additional terminal or two will be negligible. For further information, contact KIS at 303-466-5471; www.kis-kiosk.com.

- **ATM.** Install an ATM. Encourage customers to linger in your establishment. You don't want them to leave early simply because they're short on cash. Also, keep customers happy; avoid the types of machines that charge a nominal transaction fee.

Top-Ten Tips for Increasing Tips

Take a proactive approach to the whole business of tips. After all, it's in the establishment's best interest to encourage customers to tip servers more generously. Unfortunately, most managers are too busy controlling tips and trying to prevent thieving to consider tipping an area of great opportunity. Think again. Here are ten ways in which employees can increase their income. Staff will thank you for it - and so will your accountant!

- **Cash in on ambiance.** Serve drinks in as relaxing and comfortable an environment as possible. Persuade your servers that it's in their best interest to pander openly to customers. A relaxed customer is a generous customer.

- **Greet customers by name.** It makes guests feel important, particularly if they are accompanied by a group of potential new customers! Guests who feel special will repay your establishment by tipping generously. Everybody's happy!

- **Anticipation.** Train servers to anticipate customers' needs. Customers shouldn't have to hang around waiting to order that next round of drinks.

- **Celebrations.** Offer regulars, or even new customers, a free drink, if you find out that it's their birthday. It's a good move for encouraging loyalty.

- **Make change in a combination of denomina-tions.** For example, if the required change is $5, never hand over a $5 bill. Break the change down into four one-dollar bills and four quarters. It can really make a difference in the size of the tip.

- **Hand over change in a certain order.** First, hand over the cents and then place the bills on top. The customer is likely to remove the last bill placed in his hand or on the table and use it as a tip instead of the coins.

- **Take tips as they're offered.** For example, a customer may place a tip on the table as soon as the server delivers the first round of drinks. If the tip is not removed immediately, with a gracious "thank you," the next round may well go un-tipped. If the first tip is still sitting on the table, the guest may be tempted not tip for the next round.

- **Attentiveness.** Open a packet of cigarettes for a customer or even offer to light the first cigarette.

- **Overpayment.** If a customer overpays by mistake, the server should point out the overpayment immediately. Honesty is always the best policy, and your establishment will reap the long-term dividends.

- **Lost property.** If a customer leaves any personal item of value behind in the bar, do everything you can to reunite the customer with his or her mislaid property as quickly as possible. Simply putting the item aside for safekeeping isn't good enough. You want to show you care. A hefty tip is the likely outcome.

Additional Bar Equipment That Will Help Reduce Costs

As well as the many computerized total control packages specifically designed to control costs in the beverage industry, there are a number of other useful tools available. The following are well worth considering:

- **Automated liquor dispensers.** Equipment such as the Raymaster Pro 100, can measure, count and report on up to 100 different brands of liquor. For further information, visit www.auper.com/Raymaster.

- **Cost-analysis spreadsheets.** "The Calculators," for example, is a package in spreadsheet format that can speed up cost analysis in your bar. It runs under Microsoft Excel and can tackle tasks such as potential profit and loss and return-on-investment calculations. See www.auper.com/calculators for more information.

- **Gun systems.** A number of manufacturers offer "gun systems." They feature handheld guns that can handle up to 48 different brands and 16 premixed cocktails. With these systems, the bartender need never touch a bottle! For additional information, refer to www.easybar.com or www.wunderbar.com.

- **Vita-Mix blenders.** These machines make great-tasting frozen drinks - fast. The bartender can preset the time that the blender runs, so a consistent drink is produced every time. Visit www.vita-mix.com for more details.

- **Portion-control pour spouts.** Available in several shot sizes, they control liquor portion size. A sensible compromise between "free pour" and "shot glass" for bars where customers expect free-pouring. The market leader is Posi-Pour (see www.atlantic-pub.com).

- **Cocktail towers.** These keyboard-operated ultrafast devices can pour perfect cocktails in less than three seconds. Up to 16 different brands of liquor, juice and soft drinks can be blended in consistent portions. For further details, visit Azbar at www.azbar-int.com/www/anglais/tourel.htm.

LAYOUT OF A TYPICAL BAR

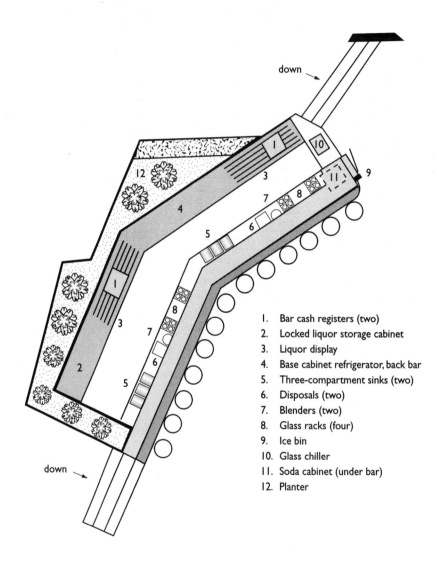

down

down

1. Bar cash registers (two)
2. Locked liquor storage cabinet
3. Liquor display
4. Base cabinet refrigerator, back bar
5. Three-compartment sinks (two)
6. Disposals (two)
7. Blenders (two)
8. Glass racks (four)
9. Ice bin
10. Glass chiller
11. Soda cabinet (under bar)
12. Planter

INDEX

G
garnish, 95, 117
glassware, 69
gross profits, 30

I
incentives, 102
Internal Revenue Service, 13
Internet, 132
inventory, 47, 52, 54, 74, 82

K
kickbacks, 38

L
labor costs, 102
last price method, 57
LIFO, 57
liquor, 54, 59, 93

M
management, 73, 83, 101, 104
markups, 25
menus, 66
Microsoft Excel, 17
mixed drinks, 68
monthly inventory, 51

N
nonalcoholic beverages, 90

O
orientation program, 104
ounce, 21

overcharging, 74
overpouring, 74

P
point-of-sale, 25
pool table, 128
portion, 21, 66
portion control, 61
pouring costs, 73
premium brands, 91
pricing, 24
pricing methods, 26
profit, 20, 97
promotions, 87
purchase order, 35, 39, 50
purchasing, 33
purchasing schedule, 35

Q
quality, 35
quantity, 49
quarters, 25

R
ratios, 64
receiving, 41
recipes, 65, 97
recruitment, 101, 111

S
sales volume, 32
security, 27, 48, 79, 116
shortchanging, 75
spillage, 22
spreadsheet, 17

staff, 101
storage, 47, 89
storeroom, 54
substitution, 75

T
target audience, 23
theft, 73, 77
time cards, 80
tips, 78, 133
training, 104, 106

U
underpouring, 75
uniforms, 129

V
vendors, 35, 40, 46

W
wastage, 67, 82
well brands, 91
well liquor, 93, 98, 130
wine, 54, 88, 119

Y
yield, 23

Z
"Z" reading, 28
zero-based budget, 11

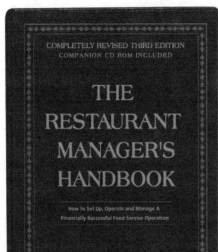

If you enjoyed this book, order the entire series!